From

Contract
to Close

| HOW TO CREATE COMPELLING HOME BUYING |
| EXPERIENCES THAT EARN REFERRALS |

JEFF SHORE

AND

BOB MIRMAN

ISBN: 978-0-9884915-7-1

Cover and page design by Six Penny Graphics.

Shore Consulting books are available at special quantity discounts to use as premiums and sales promotions or for use in corporate training programs. To contact a representative, please visit the Contact page at www.jeffshore.com or call +1 844-54-SHORE.

Table of Contents

SECTION 1:
Contact to Contract

SECTION 2:
Charting the Progress

SECTION 3:
The Crucial 60 Days

SECTION 4:
After Move-In

About the Authors

Jeff Shore

Jeff Shore is the founder and president of Shore Consulting, Inc. a company specializing in field-tested and proven consumer psychology-based sales training programs. Jeff is a top-selling author and an award-winning keynote speaker. He holds the prestigious Certified Speaking Professional designation from the National Speakers Association and is a member of the NSA's exclusive Million Dollar Speakers Group.

With over 30 years of real-world, frontline experience, Jeff's advanced sales strategies spring from extensive research into the psychology of buying and selling. He teaches salespeople how to climb inside the minds of their customers to sell the way their buyers want to buy. Using these modern, game-changing techniques, Jeff Shore's clients generated over $54 billion in sales last year.

Jeff lives in the idyllic town of Newcastle, California, with his wife, Karen. When he isn't on an airplane or in front of an audience, you'll find Jeff doting on his tribe of granddaughters, serving at his church, or getting some ice time at the local rink where he plays in a competitive hockey league.

jeffshore.com

Bob Mirman

 Bob Mirman founded National Survey Systems in 1984, changing the name to Eliant in 2002. He was the first to create a national system for benchmarking homebuyers' ratings of their new home purchase and ownership experience. Bob and the Eliant team have assisted over 1,600 homebuilders, lenders, and escrow firms in the U.S., Canada, and the Middle East to deliver extraordinary customer experiences that drive sales from referrals.

Completing a clinical psychology internship in the Michigan state hospital system, Bob moved on to the psychology PhD program at the University of Kansas, leaving there to work for a large consulting company specializing in motivating Fortune 500 sales and production teams to make strong performance improvements based on behavioral psychology principles.

Bob and his wife, Martha, live in Pinehurst, North Carolina, and are avid golfers, but Bob's real passion is serving as Martha's caddy in her major tournaments all over the country.

eliant.com

Foreword

THE PROFESSION OF SALES—when approached correctly and with a focus on bringing immense value to one's customer—is perhaps the most righteous element of business, and for a number of reasons.

First and foremost, the sales profession helps another human being acquire something they need, want, or desire, something that will improve the quality of their life.

Economically, not only does the sale provide income and profit for the company (allowing them to continue in business), but it also enables them to provide employment for more individuals and their families. By extension (through the money these families will spend), the community—and ultimately the entire economic system—will benefit.

This, however, doesn't mean that sales itself—either the process leading up to it, or (as we learn in this fantastic book) the process that follows it—is necessarily handled correctly and properly. All too often it isn't…much to the detriment of all parties involved.

In *From Contract to Close*, authors Jeff Shore and Bob Mirman challenge readers to broaden the definition of "salespeople" to include all those who directly interact with the customer. From builders to superintendents to design center staff to warranty representatives, Jeff and Bob splendidly illustrate that when it comes to customer care, everyone is in sales!

Full disclosure: I've been a huge fan of Jeff's for a long, long time. The man has proven himself not only to be among the best sales professionals and sales teachers in the world, but he is also one of the finest, most genuine, most caring human beings I've ever had the pleasure to meet. In my opinion, Jeff Shore represents everything good about business, sales, and most importantly, humanity. I am thrilled to see his body of work broadening to include all the customer-facing team members in the business.

Although I've only gotten to know Bob through this book, it does not surprise me one bit that he and Jeff have partnered on this extraordinary project. Bob's background and work (and the examples from his company's work shared in the book) are most impressive and inspirational.

Like a tale of two cities, *From Contract to Close* is the tale of two couples who are similar in many ways, wanting to buy similar homes in similar neighborhoods. Not similar, however, is one thing: the customer experiences they had in buying their new home and the ensuing follow-through process. And that one thing actually meant everything!

Not only did it mean everything to the two families; it will also dictate the eventual results and future business of the two builders. One will have their name disparaged, and the other will receive word-of-mouth marketing that advertising dollars simply cannot buy, resulting in tons of referrals and additional qualified prospects.

Neither of the above results happens in a vacuum, however. There is a reason for it. That reason includes a system.

I personally define a system as "the process of predictably achieving a goal based on a logical and specific set of how-to principles." The key is predictability. If a methodology has proven to be successful (as Jeff and Bob's has), then following the system will basically yield the same positive results.

Systems though, especially in the context of customer experiences, depend upon people who care and genuinely have in their hearts the well-being of those they serve. Even the greatest system in the world will be worthless if it's seen by its users as an "end in and of itself" rather than as a benevolent mechanism to serve others.

The authors provide the system. It's up to you (the home building professional) to care, and the managers to ensure that these are the kinds of people they are inviting to be part of their team.

So aside from sharing a system and methodology for immense success, *From Contract to Close* proves a very important lesson: While service itself is always about the customer, the experience is dependent upon the service providers. Successful companies (and their leadership teams) create a culture, comprised of a benevolent system, in which the customer feels safe, comfortable, cared for…and which they will treasure.

The result will not be a "satisfied" customer, but an ECSTATIC customer—one who feels excited to tell everyone they know about the spectacular team and organization they worked with, as well as the unique and magnificent experience they received.

With the help of the superb teaching in this book, YOU can be that spectacular service provider.

I wish you Stratospheric Success!

Bob Burg
Coauthor of *The Go-Giver* and author of *Endless Referrals*

Introduction

THE BEST HOME BUILDERS aren't *looking* for referrals; they are providing great experiences that *earn* referrals. The best home builders aren't looking for great evaluation scores; they are providing great experiences that *earn* great evaluation scores.

This book is not about what we get from our customers; it is about what we *earn* from our customers. We all want more referral sales, but only top home builders run their organization in a manner that earns those referrals. Top home builders gain over 40% of their new sales through referrals, and that comes from providing world-class service.

Of course, every home builder aims to deliver a customer experience that is smooth, efficient, and enjoyable. All too often that journey ends up rough, complicated, and arduous.

What are the secrets to an extraordinary home buying experience? That is the question we propose to answer in the pages that follow.

This book centers around the story of two fictional (and yet all-too-realistic) homebuyers, two friends who purchase at the same time from two different home builders. The book follows their journey from purchase to move-in and beyond. Along the way we will learn how one home builder succeeds in delivering an enjoyable experience, while the other suffers because of inferior customer care practices.

Each chapter unfolds the story a bit more, while offering insights and best practices at every turn. And each chapter concludes with specific recommendations for application ideas.

Here is the challenge. Don't just *read* this book! Use it as an opportunity to grow and improve by first evaluating your current practices and then finding new ways to improve and enhance the buyer journey.

We believe this is an important and appropriate read for every customer-facing employee working for any home builder. Everyone in the organization should be in lockstep when it comes to the clarity and communication of each message sent.

The suggestions and practices herein were not invented out of thin air. They come from decades of new home research and experiences. The authors have worked closely with home builders who have delivered millions of homes in all kinds of markets. We have seen the very best and very worst of execution in customer care. We have personally witnessed customers who have shed tears of joy; we have also seen customers cry out of sheer frustration.

Ultimately, we all desire to achieve the same important goal: homebuyers who are ecstatic about their new home experience and willing to passionately describe the journey to their friends.

Let's get started!
Jeff and Bob

Prologue

The Homebuyers' Story

TO SAY THAT JANET AND KYLIE were inseparable from childhood would be a drastic understatement. It took all of two weeks after Kylie's family moved to Janet's hometown of Ashmont before the two became best friends.

Going to college together was a given. Vacationing together was an annual ritual.

For anyone else, the very idea of best friends marrying twin brothers would seem highly improbable. For Janet and Kylie it made perfect sense.

And so it would come as no surprise that when Janet and her husband Matt decided to purchase a brand-new home, Kylie and her husband Craig would find themselves shopping in the same part of town. In fact, the two couples decided on homes in adjoining housing developments within the same master plan community. They were determined that one day their children would play in the same neighborhood park.

This is a story of two homebuyers and two home builders. It's also a story of great joy and tremendous heartache, of success and regret.

Welcome to Ashmont Farms.

SECTION 1:

Contact to Contract

Chapter One

Home Shopping

NEITHER JANET NOR KYLIE was particularly displeased with where they lived, but both had plans to start a family; the school system was of paramount importance. Their collective journey brought them to two adjoining developments within the Ashmont Farms master planned community. The friends were convinced that one day their kids would attend Ashmont Elementary together.

"One thing I love about Ashmont Farms," said Janet, "is that there are several builders all within walking distance to one another, and all centered around the new regional park and playground."

Kylie said, "It's scary how we think so much alike. We've been online looking at the builders in that community and we were really drawn to the Matchless Homes neighborhood. We toured the homes a couple of days ago. The floor plans are incredible. And the salesperson has been sending us really interesting information about the market, design trends, all kinds of things."

"We looked at Matchless Homes and really liked what we saw. I think we're leaning more toward the Connor Gregory community," said Janet. "Matt loves the oversized yards and I think the streetscape is spectacular."

Kylie asked, "How serious are you? I mean, are you ready to buy?"

"I think so," replied Janet. "It's really everything we're looking for."

Within a few days the two families had appointments with their respective builders to talk about the floor plan and to pick out the ideal homesite.

Janet and Kylie spoke regularly about the process. They shared both the joy and the fear that, as it turned out, both friends carried in abundance.

Homebuyer Insights

"The amount of information that we needed to process was so overwhelming. Our salesperson did a great job of prioritizing what was really important—what we really needed to focus on."

Insights

This is not a book about sales technique, but we would be remiss if we didn't emphasize the importance of deeply understanding the customer's history, their motivation, the areas of dissatisfaction with their current home, and an idea of what they want the future to look like. This information will be invaluable throughout the process for all involved.

We recommend the robust usage of a customer relationship management (CRM) system to actively capture the important details of the customers' lives. But the real benefit is when that data is easily accessible for every member of the Community Team.

As such, sales professionals should not hoard that valuable homebuyer information. Sharing customer insights with the rest of the Community Team (construction, warranty, design, mortgage) will provide both context and empathy throughout the entire process. If you don't already have a systematic method of conveying homebuyer profiles to all of the Community Team members, put one in place immediately.

Set the tone for positive emotional engagement from the start and continue that throughout the process. The entire Community Team should be committed to providing a positive emotional experience. Your customer desires to have an upbeat conversation with every employee. The mental approach of Community Team members is critical to relational success.

Home Builder How-To

A prospective purchaser, and even someone who pulls the "I'm just looking" card, deserves us at our very best. Why? Because they have friends and family that they will report back to about their experience, and even if they aren't purchasing right now, they will be eventually, and we want to be top of mind.

Kaylie Austin, Division Sales Manager

Community Teams

Throughout the book we will reference "Community Teams." These teams are comprised of every customer-facing employee operating a community (including, but not limited to, salespeople, construction superintendent, studio designer, customer care representative, etc.). It's imperative that the Community Team members are on the same page and deliver consistent messages to the customer.

We recommend weekly Community Team meetings to talk about the journey of every customer in backlog, and also to talk about any strong prospects who could soon make a purchase decision. Each team member should be intricately familiar with the journey of every customer.

Understanding the Customer's "Emotional Altitude"

Let's get you familiar with a term you will see throughout this book: Emotional Altitude. Emotional Altitude is a gauge of the customer's *positive* emotional experience throughout the process, measured on a spectrum of low to high.

By way of example, Emotional Altitude for many home-buyers is quite high when selecting a home or a homesite. However, it wanes when filling out mortgage applications. Emotional Altitude will rise and fall throughout the process.

It's critical to understand that customers often base their Emotional Altitude on what they see or hear (or don't see or hear) from the homebuilder's Community Team.

In short, Emotional Altitude is modeled by Community Team members. The amount of positive energy they actively bring into every conversation will be adopted by the customer. Carry that upbeat energy into every interaction. Every bit of communication matters. Communicate frequently, helpfully, and always with a positive tone.

Application

- Create a system by which Community Team members have easy access to homebuyer profile information. Understanding the customer's mission, their motivation, their wants and their needs will go a long way toward establishing empathy.

- Create an environment where Community Teams work closely together at every stage of the process. Weekly Community Team meetings will help build a foundation of customer care. These team meetings should be dedicated to understanding the needs, issues, and communication patterns for every customer. If you haven't established a clearly defined Community Team program, start there.

- Establish an *internal* culture of customer respect, starting with the language and tone of voice used when discussing customer issues. The leadership team cannot speak in harsh and demeaning tones about their customers and then expect Community Teams to care for these homebuyers with care and empathy.

Group Discussion Questions

1. Think back to a pair of similar customers who started their home buying journey at the same time. How was their customer care alike and how was it different from the beginning?

2. Create a list of team members who will come in contact with a customer during their home buying journey. Do all of these individuals know how to access buyer information in your CRM? What are the benefits of doing so?

3. At what frequency do you have Community Team meetings? Weekly? Bi-Weekly? Monthly? Who (person or department) typically is not included in these meetings but should be?

4. Think of a recent customer's home buying journey. Identify the two highest and two lowest points for their Emotional Altitude during the journey.

Chapter Two

The Home and Homesite Selection

KYLIE CALLED JANET with the exciting update. "Craig and I are getting very close to purchasing in the Matchless Homes neighborhood. We have absolutely fallen in love with a floor plan that is flexible enough to change things around when we have kids. I'm scared…and thrilled."

Janet and Matt were in a similar position at Connor Gregory.

Janet replied, "We really want to be in by the end of summer and our salesperson basically guaranteed that they could do that. The model home we saw is just beautiful and we love the attention to detail."

"So do you think you're going to move forward with it?" asked Kylie.

"I think so. I want to sign the contract today but Matt is a little bit reluctant."

"Why is that?" asked Kylie.

Janet replied, "He wanted to ask some questions of the construction superintendent, but the salesperson told him that the superintendent is really busy and that's not really the way they work. He just said that when the home gets delivered 'it's going to be perfect, trust me.' It always raises a red flag for Matt when a salesperson says the words 'trust me.'"

"Interesting," replied Kylie. "We already met our construction superintendent. Our salesperson had her come out to the homesite with us while we were looking at lots."

"Wow," said Janet. "That's impressive. We just walked the community with a map and selected the lot we liked the best. Matt wanted to do that without the salesperson; he doesn't like being pressured."

"Hmm, it didn't feel like pressure to me," replied Kylie. "It just felt like they really cared. And she warned us of some of the things that often go wrong with the building of a brand-new home. That actually made us feel more confident in the decision. I know it sounds weird but the team at Matchless Homes seemed genuinely excited about the journey we're on. We kind of adopted their enthusiasm, I guess."

"Sounds nice," said Janet. "So, what's next?"

"Craig wanted to go over some of the details and I want to talk to our financial planner about the move. Our salesperson made an appointment for us to come back the day after tomorrow. What's next for you?"

Janet replied, "The ball is in our court. I want to buy today. It will take me a couple of days to convince Matt that he wants to buy as well."

"Good luck with that!"

Homebuyer Insights

"It's such a big decision. This affects our entire life. To be handed a map and told 'go help yourself' was cold and a bit rude. Isn't this the job of the salesperson? Am I missing something?"

Insights

The selection of the floor plan and homesite sets in motion a critical aspect of success in customer care: setting proper expectations. Too many sales professionals believe that expectation-setting begins at the time of contract. We disagree.

Good salespeople focus (appropriately) on making the sale. The aim is to sell a new home to every willing prospect who visits the community. Unfortunately, too many sales-people are so focused on getting the sale that they miss the opportunity to set proper expectations. The desire to just get the sale is overwhelming...and distasteful.

We call this "Commission Breath" and, like halitosis, it's an unattractive affliction for all involved. There's room at every moment for respect and professionalism, and that includes the way in which we set expectations.

Homebuyer Insights

"Our agent was responsible for our deciding to purchase here. From choosing our lot to keeping us on budget in the selection process, he was our guiding light."

Getting it Wrong

Setting inaccurate expectations, by commission or omission, can create significant problems down the road. Poor expectation setting and poorly worded promises by the salesperson can end up throwing the superintendent and/or customer service representative under the bus. Ultimately, the customer will pay the price.

Phrases like these will cause nothing but problems:

- *"We'll definitely have you moved in by this (specific) date."*

- *"Your home should be in perfect condition by your final walk-through."*

- *"Our customer service team will respond immediately to your call."*

Too often, in a misguided effort to convert the prospect to a buyer, small exaggerations in the expected deliverable can occur. In such cases, buyer assumptions are inadvertently (or purposely) left uncorrected.

Home Builder How-To

After interviewing (discovery), start with the map. Maps are cool and a forgotten resource and using it as such makes things immediately interesting. Maps can be paper or expensive three-dimensional like your old HO train set when you were a kid. It doesn't matter what kind of map, if you're a good story teller and can make a map come alive. Maps and taking a brief minute to apply effort and respect—allowing your buyer to calibrate and become oriented to the greater surroundings—sets the location stage. It's critical. Not doing this robs the buyer of not only confirming a great overall community location…but also discovering a few selected site locations within the community—and getting excited.

Patrick Crocetta, Vice President of Sales and Marketing

Getting it Right

Great salespeople avoid giving off "Commission Breath" via a different mindset. While the immediate goal in selling a home is always in play, these *great* salespeople own a more sophisticated—and company-oriented—long-term perspective.

You see, the end game goal is not to simply create a *home-buyer*. The true end game is to create elated homeowners: customers who are so thrilled with both the home and the purchase experience that they would absolutely recommend both the salesperson and the homebuilder to a friend.

The salesperson is charged with maintaining a positive energy environment throughout the process, but not by overpromising. The objective is to raise and sustain the customer's Emotional Altitude, that measure of positive emotional experience during the buying process.

Establishing Trust

Great salespeople recognize that the best sales opportunities happen when prospects trust them. Trust is earned by being consistently honest and transparent:

- Making realistic promises and consistently meeting if not *beating* their promises most of the time.

- Communicating bad news immediately.

- Asking questions of the prospect and listening carefully to the response.

- Nicely saying "No" to the homebuyer's request when it's appropriate to do so.

- Proactively communicating ALL the news and status reports—good, bad, and ugly—in a consistently timely manner.

These great salespeople recognize the value of teamplay to the long-term success of the building organization. There are no silos here; all the departments are interconnected. The success of each department is contingent on the performance of all the other departments. Construction can never achieve "Excellent" customer ratings if salespeople and studio designers promise more than construction can actually deliver.

Application

- Get your salespeople meeting with each other to role play the best way to phrase realistic promises so that they can see how others are effectively setting appropriate expectations while keeping the buyer's emotion strong and positive.

- Have your salespeople shadow each other during actual presentations. Let them see what it looks like to raise the homebuyer's Emotional Altitude level as the sales conversation leads to a purchase decision.

- Create a list of words and phrases that should never be used with a customer. Things like, "perfect," "immediate response," "guarantee," etc.

- Select one to two field representatives from each department (sales, design, construction, and customer care) to participate in the Expectations Management Team. This group should be responsible for creating a list of the expectations and promises which field representatives should be comfortable in communicating with buyers. The wording for these promises should be role-played and practiced by all representatives, so that all team members are making the same promises, using the same terminology. These are the only promises that should be allowed!

Group Discussion Questions

1. What are two scenarios that have led to customers having unrealistic expectations? How did you address them?

2. Does your construction superintendent accompany each homebuyer on a site walkthrough? If not, why not? If so, what are his or her key objectives during this interaction with the buyers?

3. The homesite selection is one of the steps in a customer's home buying journey where their Emotional Altitude is high. What can you do with your construction superintendent and other Community Team members to help them reinforce the high?

4. What would you do if you overheard someone on your team making an unrealistic promise to a customer?

Chapter Three

Expectation Management Pre-Contract

JANET WAS EXCITED. Her husband, Matt, was more skeptical. Matt owned an auto body repair shop and he knew firsthand the danger in making guarantees on both delivery dates and finish quality. Words like "perfect" always raised a red flag with him.

Janet was undeterred in her conversation with Kylie.

"If we buy this weekend, we can get this home built and ready by September 1st. The salesperson assured me that they're really good about meeting their dates without delay. Matt is skeptical, but then Matt is always skeptical."

"Wow," Kylie replied. "Our salesperson was not nearly as optimistic. She was talking about the possibility of supply chain issues and the fact that the city is sometimes slow in the inspection process. I'd like to move by the end of summer but we were told we should be flexible with that date. We'll make it work though, one way or another."

"Yeah, I get it," said Janet. "Stuff happens. But I'm also excited about living in a home that's perfect when you move in. Not like when we moved into the home we're in now—it was gross."

"Did you say 'perfect'?" asked Kylie. "Your salesperson didn't use that word, right? Because our salesperson was very clear: 'It won't be absolutely perfect at move-in, but we'll make it right.'"

"So, are you going to buy it?" asked Janet.

"Craig is ready. He really likes the construction superintendent. He loved that there was a very frank conversation telling us that things *will* go wrong along the way—windows that get broken, rain delays, that sort of thing. But she assured us that there's always a process in place to correct those things as they come up. I think we're ready."

"Can you believe it?" said Janet. "We're going to go through this together. This is awesome!"

"Let's keep comparing notes. I'm excited for the journey."

Homebuyer Insights

"I was told my home would take about six months to build. It ended up taking almost 12 months to close, so I had to pay extra for month-to-month rent. I would have signed a year lease instead."

Insights

An important part of the selling process includes the act of explaining the purchase and construction process, often in response to questions raised by the customer. That discussion will include topics like projected build times, expected finish quality, major milestones, communication patterns with key employees, etc.

Note that all of this is happening while the salesperson is still attempting to procure the sale. Salespeople must strike a balance between moving the customer toward a purchase decision, on the one hand, and setting realistic expectations on the other.

The challenge and opportunity is to under-promise on the deliverables without devaluing the offering or striking fear into the hearts of buyers.

Begin by eliminating words that will erode trust if they're not met:

- *"Perfect"*

- *"Absolute"*

- *"Ideal"*

- *"Guarantee"*

- *"Definitely"*

One slip-up in the execution will cause these words to come back to haunt the entire team.

The better approach is to create a "Promise List"—a cooperative effort by sales/design center/construction/customer care representatives to identify a master list (complete with script) of the key promises all staff will make and then live up to. All team members must be on the same page!

Let's take a look at some data from Eliant's continuous collection of new-home buyers' evaluations of their purchase and ownership experience. This is based on over 200,000 Move-In, Mid-Year, and Year-End evaluations administered each year to the customers of almost 200 home builder clients.

Eliant's All-Client average score for *"Builder met its promises/commitments"* has been very steady, averaging over 85% for the last 12 years, hitting its high point of 86% in 2020 (the first year of COVID-19). In that year, homebuyers were forced to deal with an entire set of rapidly changing realities. Supply shortages, waiting lists, and rising prices became the new normal. A great deal of grace was offered by home buyers. "We get it—it's a weird situation and we just want a new home."

By 2021, homebuyers began to tire of the continuous excuses and poorly conceived promises for late deliveries and diminishing levels of service. Home builders' customer ratings of "Builder Met Commitments" dropped to an all-time low of 83%, a significant decline in a short period of time.

For a population of survey respondents in the tens of thousands, just a small 0.5% change is statistically significant. So, this drop from 86% to 83% (3%) represents a major shift in homebuyers' confidence with home builders' ability to make reasonable promises...and to keep their promises.

Part of this drop is to be expected. Home builders were taken by surprise about the severity and continuing duration of the supply-chain derailment. But make no mistake: Regardless of the difficult reality of supply chain delays, the home builder's entire team must respond with increasing transparency, honesty, humility, and more realistic promise-making.

Home Builder How-To

One technique I encourage our salespeople to adopt and develop is "inoculating" homebuyers against future stress and negative emotions (because they're inevitable in the customer journey), during the early periods of low stress and high positive emotion.

The prime example is at contract signing, when it's typical for homebuyers to be absolutely giddy over the great and life-changing decision we've just placed in motion. It takes guts and practice for a salesperson to artfully swerve out of a smiles-and-handshakes celebration and say, "Now, just so you know, it's not *always* going to feel like this, but we've got you the whole way, anyway! This process is pretty well known to be a roller coaster ride. Instead of riding it with you, we're going to stay here on the ground and get you to the finish safely! SO, when you call me, freaking out about something, anything, I'm going to be here for you, just like I am now, and we're going to work through it. I'll remind you of this conversation, and show you that we've got you!"

Pete Lange, Sales Team Leader

Application

Test your teams. What are they saying now? Listen through the ears of a homebuyer; they tend to listen for what they want to hear. What are the potential trouble spots? If you are an Eliant client, read through the "Buyer Comments

Report" and search for key words and phrases like "delay,"
"expectations," promise," "unhappy," and "dissatisfied."
  Phrases to utilize:

- *"In this environment, delays are likely."*

- *"We are estimating a delivery date of (x), but delays
  should absolutely be expected in this economy."*

- *"I can't promise a specific date, but I can promise to
  keep you updated."*

- *"Here is our schedule for communicating your anticipated delivery date…"*

Here is a list of the **10 expectations** home builders
should be setting with every new homebuyer:

1. The likelihood of variance on delivery date

2. Frequency and timing of communication from the
   builder about key dates

3. The reason for and necessity of adhering to cut-off
   dates; who is ultimately responsible for meeting these
   deadlines?

4. Anticipated condition of home at final orientation
   and likelihood of a "punch list"

5. Anticipated time to clear the punch list

6. Likelihood of the need for warranty repairs after move-in

7. Typical speed of response to repair requests

8. Probability that many types of repairs require more than one visit to complete

9. Likelihood of visible changes to the home due to settling over time

10. Benefits of homeowner maintenance and which items are the homeowner's responsibility

Assemble a team of customer-centric team members and have them write out suggested language for each of these expectations. Get the entire team working on how to deliver these messages in a consistent, direct yet positive tone.

Group Discussion Questions

1. What is the longest home delivery timeline you've ever had? How did you keep the customer informed through the process? What could you have done better?

2. If a customer threatens to walk away when you can't commit to a specific delivery date, what can you do?

3. How does providing realistic expectations for delivery
   date and move-in quality help the customer? How
   does it help your Community Team?

Chapter Four

Contract and Celebration

NOT SURPRISINGLY, given the symmetry of their lives, Kylie and Janet signed purchase agreements within hours of one another.

"I'm excited and exhausted," reported Kylie when the two friends met for an early evening walk.

"Not me," said Janet. "Matt read through the contract and just emailed the salesperson whenever he had questions."

"Wait, you didn't meet with the salesperson to go over all that stuff?"

"Nope," replied Janet. "It was all DocuSign. Matt worked on it for a quite a while but he got it done. He was getting pretty frustrated with all the legal mumbo jumbo, but I just let him handle all that."

"Wow, that's interesting. Craig and I met with the sales-person for over two hours."

"What took two hours?" asked Janet.

"Going over the contract, meeting a couple of team members, walking through the home buying process…all kinds of stuff. It was exhausting but it was really informative. We walked away knowing so much more about what to expect. You didn't get any of that?"

"Not really," Janet replied. "I mean, the salesperson told us the time frame and talked about some inspections along the way. Then he told us to make an appointment with the lender and the design studio. That was that."

"Hmm, our salesperson made those appointments for us. Oh, and at the end they gave us this really cool key chain in like a jewelry box. Something to look forward to when we get the keys to the home. It was really sweet."

"Good for you. At the end of the day, I just want a nice home, and I think we're getting that."

Homebuyer Insights

"Our salesperson took our picture signing the contract. She gave us a nice bottle of wine when we finished. It was a nice touch."

Insights

Is the contract signing simply a matter of paperwork and facts? Or is there room to heighten the Emotional Altitude to further cement the sale and to use this as a time for celebration?

Buyer's remorse is real, and it begins to set in almost immediately. The sheer magnitude of the decision and the long-term nature of the commitment can cause immediate and palpable angst.

What can be done at the time of contract to cement the emotional connection to the home? And how can the salesperson set realistic expectations without diminishing the buyer's enthusiasm?

Home Builder How-To

Memorialize the moment: Alisha stopped by the dollar store and grabbed balloons and stuck them in the back of her car, because she knew it would be the day this family said yes! Once they signed the contract, she took them back out to the home site to celebrate and then sent their kiddo home with the balloons. Total investment = $4

Chelsea Timmons, Vice President of Community Experience

Where is the Coaching?

Are front-line sales professionals handling the contract appointment properly? Are they saying the right things, and in the way that the sales leader wants them said? Too often we cannot answer this important question.

The reality is that sales managers rarely see or hear what happens in the contract-writing process. They're not present to observe the tone and energy. Nor can they hear how the process is being explained and what expectations are being set (or not set!)

This has always been the case in a home building environment in which, more commonly than not, the salesperson exists in a satellite sales center, far from the sales leader's office. Absent a concerted effort to be present at a contract signing, the sales manager is left to assume that the promises made and expectations set are clear, accurate, and appropriate.

Quite obviously, there exists a potential point of failure in such an arrangement.

The Celebration

Let's start by addressing the issue of sustained Emotional Altitude. There is an opportunity here that is too often missed.

Question: How does your customer celebrate their decision?

Oh, they do. But is that celebration initiated by the salesperson, or is this something they do alone at dinner?

The celebration should be a planned event as a part of the contract signing. Even a small celebratory act raises the Emotional Altitude and further cements the homebuyer's decision. This will be vitally important when, inevitably, things go wrong.

Think of the celebration as an investment into the emotional bank account; think of an error in the process as a withdrawal. You never want to be overdrawn!

It doesn't take much. We encourage you to brainstorm this with your team and let them own the ideas. It might be an introduction and round of applause from the Community Team. Perhaps a small gift—providing an empty and builder-branded key chain with the promise of delivering the actual key several months from now.

Whatever you do, make it a moment they'll remember. Cement the sale by cementing the emotion.

Home Builder How-To

Our success includes some simple practices. Every customer enjoys the process and celebration of peak moments...

- Contract celebration includes a photo session at their home or jobsite and posts on social media with their approval.
- Call from the home builder within 24 hours of contract to congratulate them and make a time to connect weekly for updates.
- Weekly calls for updates.
- Trim signing is everyone's favorite moment. We invite them to write a message on their studs or floors to bless the home or simply write themselves a message that is always in the home. This is another photo and social media moment.
- We also have a closing celebration where we literally roll out a red carpet. We deliver the keys and take a photo of them opening their front door for the first time. We have about two to three employees there to celebrate with them.
- Within the first 30 days of move-in we make a call to them to see how things are going and if there is anything we can do to help them get settled.
- We send cards on their house anniversary signed by all of our leadership team.

Kristi Pinnick, Vice President of Sales and Design

Explaining the Process

The next consideration is how to give the customer something of a road map of the process. Most homebuyers are clueless as to the specifics on what happens next. But giving them a flyover will provide context for all the details they're about to hear.

Script this out and rehearse it over and over again. "Let me explain the process at the very high level and then we can get into some of the detail. It all starts today with the contract signing. Then we make an appointment to…"

Try to keep this overview down to 90 seconds or so. Too much time means you're sharing too much micro detail. Providing the buyer with a graphic picture of the journey from contract to close to customer service also helps.

Once the contract is signed, the real business of transparency becomes primary. Customers deserve to know precisely how the process works.

This explanation of the journey should have been set up during pre-contract expectation setting; the buyer should not now be surprised with your honest (and more detailed) statements about the probability of delays, for example. Honesty is your primary process, and creating trust is the expected result.

The #1 thing new homebuyers want to know at or before contract is *"When can I move my family into our new home?"*

Your Expectations Management Team—comprised of one to two representatives from each department (sales, design, construction, warranty service)—should develop a written training document specifically laying out the response which every customer-facing representative of the home builder will offer when asked this question by a homebuyer.

Here is an example (and there are many variations of this schedule):

- At contract, specify the three-month window for a likely move-in.

- At trenching, narrow this down to a 45-day window.

- At drywall, narrow this down to a 1-week window.

- At the installation of counter tops, identify the expected day of final walk-through—but also remind the buyer that all types of delays are still possible, including delays in the mortgage and escrow process.

Remind the homebuyers of the critical need for compliance with the following items:

1. ALL design cutoffs, and the likely consequence of missing these dates.

2. Last-minute scheduling for initial and final walk-through (if applicable).

3. The likelihood that some items may not be completed in time for the move-in, but that these items will be completed within 30 days after move-in (or 45 or 60 days: Select a promise that you are CERTAIN your team will be able to BEAT).

We are throwing a lot at you, and that means you will be throwing a lot at your customer. Two ideas:

1. Put this down in writing and give it to your buyer at the time of contract signing. There is no way they will remember everything you tell them; having a written record will remind them of the important stuff.

2. Take your time and deliver the message in a calm way. If you see your customer starting to get over-whelmed, call a coffee break. We want this to be a pleasant experience, not a painful ordeal.

Application

Let's start with the important "big picture" ideal: Don't fall into the trap of making promises to impress the buyer; let your *actions* impress the buyer. That is a mantra that must be taught to and adopted by everyone in the organization. From there, some specific application ideas:

- Plan the celebration in advance. Make it fun and memorable. Let the team brainstorm simple and creative ways to memorialize the moment.

- Have a checklist of appropriate and accurate talking points regarding expectations.

- Look for "Planned Surprises" at contract signing to create a memorable experience. Contract signing is one of every buyer's biggest life events. Make it MEMORABLE. Take a photo of the buyer(s) holding up their contract; print the photo and immediately place it in an inexpensive frame and hand it to the buyer(s).

• Have a photo of the buyer's home or homesite ready. Ask the buyer to call the children, best friends, or significant other via FaceTime while holding up the signed contract and a picture of their new home.

Group Discussion Questions

1. What would you do if a homebuyer insisted on handling their contract review alone and signing virtually? How could you make it a meaningful and memorable event for the homebuyer?

2. How does a contract signing celebration impact the salesperson and other staff members? Who should be involved?

3. Where is the best place to have a mini-celebration when a customer signs a contract?

4. Besides expectation talking points, what else might you include on a checklist for contract signing?

Chapter Five

Introducing the Community Team

"SO," JANET BEGAN, "We're both really doing this! How are you feeling now?"

Kylie was exuberant in her response. "We just got back from the sales office and we had so much fun. It's like we're already one big happy family. We had such a good time meeting the Community Team!"

"Community Team?" replied a confused Janet. "What team are you talking about?"

"Everyone! The construction superintendent, the studio designer, the customer care representative. We talked to all of them and loved the conversation. I just get the feeling that they truly love what they do. How are you feeling?"

"Oh, yeah…good," replied Janet half-heartedly.

"Come on, Janet. What's going on?"

"To be honest, we've been dealing with some buyer's remorse. I mean, we still love the home but it's such a big commitment and we don't want to make a mistake."

"Janet, that's totally normal. Craig and I felt pretty anxious for a couple of days. But then we met the Community Team and we feel like we're on this marvelous journey together. I know it sounds silly, but it just feels like family. We really trust these people to build us a great home."

"That's the thing," replied Janet. "We've never met anyone other than the salesperson. He says he'll be the go-between and that he'll provide all the updates. I'd love to meet someone else in the organization; I think it would make us feel better. We drove through the neighborhood and it was pretty disheveled. One construction guy yelled at us and told us we needed to leave. It just got Matt and me thinking we had better keep an eye on things."

"You're not going to back out, are you?"

"I don't know. I guess what frustrates me the most is that it seems like no one from the home builder would really care if we did, other than the salesperson who loses his commission."

Insights

The level of trust in the Community Team members translates into perceptions about quality, value, and experience. Confidence in the team is critical to what should be the goal of every team member: reducing the buyer's anxiety.

Anxious homebuyers are more likely to be uncomfortable, challenging, demanding, even angry. "Comfortable" (i.e. trusting) buyers are easier to work with and are far more accepting of delays, problems, and the inevitable bumps in the building road.

Customers feel better—and more confident with their home builder—when they actually meet the Community

Team members, begin forming relationships, and believe that company representatives are kind, empathetic, conscientious, and absolutely committed to providing a high-quality home, a better-than-expected level of service, and a delightful purchase experience.

In fact, much of the consternation that arises later in the process stems from not developing a trust relationship early in the process.

The "handoff" from sales to design studio/construction/customer care is a critical component in the development of trusting relationships that drive homebuyer satisfaction and willingness to refer the home builder to a friend.

Homebuyer Insights

"Before we had even finished signing the contract we had met our builder in person and our designer over Zoom. That opportunity to talk to real people made us so comfortable about the decision."

The Power of Emotional Endorsement

Homebuyers desperately want to trust the people who will help them make their housing dream come true. When salespeople do their job properly, trust is an important result. But how does that trust transfer from sales to other department representatives?

The answer lies in what we call "Emotional Endorsement." This is not about simply introducing a Community

Team member by name, but offering a passionate commendation that this person can be trusted as the expert they are. This results in a transference of trust.

Think of it this way: Your best friend says, "You have got to see this movie. It's the best movie I've seen in years—maybe in my entire life!" That is not just a recommendation; that is Emotional Endorsement. If you trust your best friend, then you will most definitely see this movie.

It works the same way with homebuyers. If the homebuyer trusts the salesperson, and the salesperson offers an Emotional Endorsement of the construction superintendent, the trust is transferred and the homebuyer adopts an initial feeling of trust for the construction superintendent.

Of course, this requires a strong and healthy culture within both the organization and the Community Team. It is exceedingly difficult to provide great care to the customer if the internal culture is disrespectful and unsupportive. Great service to your external customers (homebuyers) should flow from the care given to your internal customers (Community Team members). In short, internal customer care = external customer care.

Making the Introductions

We recommend that the salesperson provide the buyer with a unique "Lifestyle Bio" of the design center consultant, loan officer and processing team, construction superintendent, and customer care representative assigned to their home. This special bio is not a resume of the representative's education or work history; it is designed to identify many of the representative's favorite activities (e.g. loves movies; coaches Little League; owns two dogs) in an effort to allow the buyer to easily identify with one or more aspects of the representative's lifestyle.

This important step helps to humanize the team member in the eyes of the customer and provides a social lubricant for quickly developing successful relationships.

The construction superintendent should be introduced to the homebuyer as soon as possible during or following contract signing. Prior to this meeting, the homebuyer should receive the Lifestyle Bio of the construction superintendent.

The design center consultant assigned to each homebuyer will probably be known to the salesperson, so—after first sending the buyer the designer's Lifestyle Bio—the salesperson can introduce the design center consultant to the homebuyer (even if virtually). Repeat for the loan officer and customer care representative.

When should each of these people be initially introduced to the new buyer?

- Loan officer: introduced immediately after contract (live or on video call, if possible).

- Design center consultant: introduced immediately after contract (live preferred, but virtually acceptable).

- Escrow manager: introduced soon after contract (virtually).

- Construction superintendent: introduced at or soon after contract (live). Can be introduced as part of the selling process.

- Customer care representative: introduced soon after contract (live).

Community Team members must be well trained on how to introduce themselves to the buyer:

1. Smile

2. Positive energy

3. Service promise (examples)

   a. Loan officer lays out the mortgage journey: *"I will be working hard to identify the best loan for your needs, at the lowest possible rate."*

   b. Construction superintendent offers a confident statement to the buyer: *"I look forward to building your new home for you."*

All Community Team members must follow the "script" for promises developed by the Expectations Management Team. And all Community Team members should be able to access the homebuyer's file to see the current estimated closing date so that all will respond in the same way to the buyer's #1 question: *"When is my move-in date?"*

Home Builder How-To

Our team has created bios of our Construction team to provide a photo and information about their Construction Manager that the Sales Consultant provides to the buyer at the time of scheduling their Build Quality Introduction (pre-start meeting). They sing that team member's praises so that the buyer feels like they know their Builder before even meeting. Our Sales Consultants also meet with their Construction Manager ahead of the meeting to inform him/her on the buyer (why they're purchasing, their story, hot buttons, etc.). Having this bridge on both sides helps to start the process off strongly.

Jaymie Catalano Dimbath, VP of Sales and Marketing

Application

- The process of introductions should be planned, clear, and consistent. Create Lifestyle Bios for all Community Team members and share with the customer early in the process.

- Set the expectation that there is always a small possibility that Community Team members will be moved to another community or will be changed for a variety of reasons. Note: This is particularly true as the community nears its sell-out mark.

- Share best practices among the different departments. Construction superintendents should hear the way other superintendents introduce themselves. Same for loan officers, design center consultants, etc.

Group Discussion Questions

1. If a Community Team member leaves the organization during the build, how will you manage the transition with your homebuyers?

2. Why is it valuable for the homebuyer to have a Lifestyle Bio for someone generally working far from the build process (e.g. the escrow manager)?

3. What role does sharing Lifestyle Bios of team members have in maintaining a homebuyer's Emotional Altitude?

SECTION 2:

◆

Charting the Progress

Chapter Six:

Communication Patterns

"**CAN WE GOLF** on Thursday instead of Friday this week?" Janet asked Kylie. "Matt and I are meeting with our tax guy about some stuff we need for the home loan."

"Can't do Thursday unless it's after 11:00. We're doing a Zoom conference with our Community Team," replied Kylie.

"What are you talking about?" asked Janet.

"Our homebuilder's Community Team. Every Thursday at 10:00 we get on a Zoom call where they provide updates and we can ask any questions. We've been doing that for the past few weeks since we signed the contract."

"What kind of updates?" Janet asked.

"Just progress reports on the construction, updates on loan processing, that kind of thing. And then I get to ask questions about the process and share any concerns. Like I didn't know why there were those long pipes sticking up in the air before they poured the foundation, that type of thing."

Janet was confused and, upon deeper reflection, disappointed. "Oh, okay," she replied. "I've not spoken to anyone other than the salesperson and the loan officer, and most of that communication has been through email. I guess I need to start calling them with my questions."

"I would," answered Kylie. "I always feel so much better after our Zoom calls."

Janet said, "I get the feeling my salesperson doesn't really want to talk. Even when I call him and leave a message, he responds over email."

"Does he send you photos of the home as it's being built?" asked Kylie.

Janet paused. "You're kidding, right? You don't really get photos."

"Absolutely. I'm going to make a scrapbook when we're done."

"Um, okay. I guess I'll make a scrapbook of all the emails I receive," said a disappointed Janet.

Homebuyer Insights

"Our sales rep made our dream come true, helped us to find the perfect model for me and my family. It was a great experience. She was on the lookout from start to finish. I never missed an update and she had all the sincerity and transparency in the middle of our process."

Insights

During the contract-to-closing period, the single biggest deficit in most home builders' process is the failure to frequently and proactively communicate construction status with homebuyers. The key phrase to keep in mind is that the salesperson or Community Team should do this, *"before the buyer has to ask."*

Consider the mental processing that occurs when a homebuyer does not hear proactively from a Community Team member. The questions go unanswered. The doubts begin to appear.

A psychological phenomenon called "catastrophizing" begins to conjure up worst-case scenarios within the homebuyer's mind. In time, the customer believes that if they don't initiate communication they'll be left entirely in the dark. Psychologists have defined the basic principle: "In the absence of information, we tend to think the worst has happened."

Furthermore, once a homebuyer is forced to point out a problem to the home builder, the Baader-Meinhof phenomenon kicks in, which causes the customer to start actively seeking and seeing problems often and repeatedly. Once that sense of needing to seek out potential problems on their own takes root, it becomes much more difficult to restore the customer's confidence.

Most of the negative comments received in Eliant's homebuyer satisfaction evaluations are about a lack of communication. Although many of these complaints mention the failure of the home builder's team members to respond in a timely fashion (or not at all) to their questions and requests, most of the "communication" complaints were about "being kept in the dark," not told about all the design options, not given sufficient and timely information about status of their home's construction or their loan's status, or only given information when the buyer posed the question.

The lack of *proactive* communication is the primary point
of failure requiring urgent improvement.

Homebuyer Insights

"Superintendent was so informative and responsive. Even
though I was 1,000 miles away, he always made me feel
close to the property. His updates and photos...were
always met with anticipation."

Lessons from Focus Groups

Let's start with some historical context on this. For the first
15 years that Eliant surveyed new-home buyers (1984 to
1999), the question was asked: *"I was kept informed of the
construction status of my home."* (This was performed on an
"Agree/Disagree" 10-point scale). The customers' ratings of
this question were not great, but they were decent. But the
distribution of scores was widely dispersed along a 10-point
scale. Homebuyer perceptions were all over the map.

After analyzing the survey responses to this question, the
focus was drawn to those buyers who answered (1) "Absolutely Satisfied" or (2) "Absolutely Dissatisfied." Customers
from these two groups were invited to attend separate focus
groups. The goal was to learn more about the reasons for
their strong opinions about this important communication
question.

Home Builder How-To

Communicate early and often! When I was on the sales floor, I would send out weekly communication updates to our buyers, their real estate agent, and their loan officer every single week via email starting from the day after contract execution through closing.

It never ceased to amaze me how many Realtors and loan officers were surprised by me including them in the weekly communication. I never realized how many sales consultants didn't include them in the weekly updates at other home builders.

By doing so, it kept everyone on the same page and I found that the Realtors and lenders would quickly become allies in the transaction and appreciated me keeping them in tune with the progress.

Jordan Brown, Area Sales Manager

It immediately became clear that the primary reason for their strong opinions came down to one thing. In fact, it was the same thing in both groups.

In the focus group consisting of "Absolutely Satisfied" buyers, Eliant found that they were very likely to have received construction status updates by their salesperson or construction superintendent *without their having to ask*. The homebuyer didn't have to chase anyone down to get this information; it was frequently provided proactively by the home builder. These homebuyers described how this type of communication created a sense of comfort, reduced anxiety, and built trust in the home builder.

In the other focus groups, for buyers who were clearly *unhappy* with the communication process, homebuyers complained about always having to track down someone to give them updated information about the progress of their home. They described the stress and anxiety that was created, with a resulting lack of trust in what was actually going on behind the scenes. They were uneasy and more likely to be uncomfortable with their home builder. Several admitted they had briefly considered canceling their contract.

Home Builder How-To

No matter how many times you think you need to set an expectation with your customer, plan on explaining it a few more times. It's easy for us to think we've been clear, but there is *a lot* that customers have to remember when purchasing a home and it's important that salespeople take responsibility for repeating themselves to ensure the message has been fully received.

Danielle Lipari-Mareth, Vice President of Sales

Changing the Question

Eliant then rewrote the original survey question by adding five words: "I was kept informed of construction status *without my having to ask*."

This reworded question, asking for a rating of the sales team's proactive status communication, raised the bar for determining homebuyers' satisfaction. Consequently, homebuyers' satisfaction levels were significantly lower overall than for the original question.

We have since determined that the concept of "Proactive Status Communication" is also applicable during any phase of the home building process that might be:

- Lengthy

- Complex

- Mysterious (i.e. a process unknown to most buyers)

- Ongoing

- Hidden from view

This includes the construction experience, design selection experience, mortgage process, and customer care experience post-closing.

The Psychology of the Uninformed

Think about the journey from your customer's viewpoint. This is one of the most important transactions of their entire life. The process is mentally all-consuming. Customers lose sleep thinking about the details, the issues, and the hopes and dreams.

But nothing keeps them awake more than the unknown. Uncertainty keeps anxiety at a high level. Customers who are not proactively informed feel very much alone and abandoned. In time, the relationship becomes adversarial. They become labeled by the builder as a "difficult buyer" simply because they are asking about things that should have been told to them in the first place.

It's true that some people are going to be difficult no matter what you do. The concern is with buyers who do not start out being difficult but are forced into a more aggressive stance in dealing with their builder simply as a self-protective act.

Application

- Determine the frequency of construction status communication. We suggest a Proactive Construction Status Update of no less than every 7 to 10 days, increasing in frequency as (1) construction progresses, or (2) the buyer becomes noticeably anxious (i.e. frequently calls to inquire about status or product deliveries).

- A single call from a buyer to inquire about construction status should be viewed as a red flag. Multiple calls from this buyer should move the buyer to an increased level of proactive status communication.

- Some builders establish set times each week for communicating status updates and tell their customers to expect an update at that time. While there is some merit to the promised predictability, there is also a reasonable argument that a predictable pattern is not the best approach. Why? Because when you meet your promise and deliver the construction updates as expected, the best you can earn is a satisfied customer; you should always aim to totally delight your buyers with just a bit more than they expected! Don't overlook the opportunity here to surprise and delight the buyer with your communication.

- The other disadvantage of a promised time and day for your update is that it is extremely difficult to continually meet this kind of promise. If you get busy or forget to make the status call, the buyer will be upset because he or she expected to hear from you.

- It's perfectly fine—and preferred—to deliver these update messages even if nothing has really happened since your last status alert: It's OK to say *"Nothing has changed since our last conversation or status report."* The non-substantive content of this message is less important than the clear impression that you are "on top" of this buyer's situation, that you are on the buyer's team, that you can be trusted to serve as the buyer's eyes and ears, and that the buyer can relax and even go on vacation knowing that the sales associate is watching over the construction of their home.

Group Discussion Questions

1. Have you ever had a homebuyer who complained about getting too much information? If so, what were they complaining about? If not, what does that indicate?

2. Besides a phone call, email, or video chat, how else can your Customer Team communicate with your homebuyer to surprise and delight them?

3. Why is it important that you keep the homebuyer's Realtor and loan agent involved in communication updates?

4. How would you deal with a homebuyer who requests daily updates?

Chapter Seven

Communication Methods

"I'M GETTING KIND OF FRUSTRATED," said Janet on her Saturday morning walk with Kylie. "The only time I ever talk to anyone at Connor Gregory Homes is when I call them. I swear that if I never called them I'd have no idea what's going on. Isn't it frustrating?"

"Well, no," said Kylie sheepishly. "We're just not having that problem. I hear from the salesperson or from other people on the team at least once a week."

Janet was incredulous. "They call you once a week?!"

"They don't always call. Sometimes it's a video recording that I receive and for small stuff I get text messages. But just yesterday we were on a FaceTime with the superintendent. She wanted to show us the placement of a couple extra outlets we had ordered for Craig's office."

"Now I'm just getting angry," said Janet. "We can't talk to our superintendent no matter what. Everything goes through the salesperson, and we don't even hear from him. It's time to let them know that this is not what good customer service looks like."

"So you haven't said anything yet?" Kylie asked.

"No. Matt keeps telling me this is 'par for the course,' and that all builders operate the same way. It sounds like your builder is a glaring exception to that rule. At this point, it's not just that I'm the one who initiates every conversation. The bigger issue is that I really want to trust my home builder and I just don't."

"I'm so sorry, Janet."

"I'm going to start asking for updates over social media, for crying out loud. Somehow, I have to get their attention."

Insights

The situation in this story is troubling on many levels, but Janet's plight is indicative of an implicit truth for homebuyers: Communication creates trust. As a corollary, a lack of communication creates a lack of trust.

Different situations call for different types of communication. In this chapter, we'll offer ideas for when to use what type of outreach (phone, video update, email, etc.). The key message is to look not for the *easiest* way to update (email) but for the *best* way to reach out, and always with the customer's best interests in mind.

The Communication Hierarchy

We've designed a helpful framework called the Communication Hierarchy, which identifies and ranks the effectiveness of different communication methods, ranging from most effective to least effective.

The Communication Hierarchy ranks in this order:

1. Face-to-face conversation

2. Video conversation (Zoom or FaceTime)

3. Phone conversation

4. Video recording

5. Voice recording / voice mail

6. Text message

7. Email

The objective is to utilize the most effective communication method appropriate to the task. When communicating significant milestones, for example, a video call is probably the best approach. For confirming that a document was received, a text message might do the trick.

For You or For Them

One piece of advice in selecting the proper communication method: Make the decision based upon what the customer needs, NOT on what makes you most comfortable.

Too many salespeople rely upon texting or emailing because it's just easier. But this isn't about doing what's easy. It's about doing what's best. Ask yourself, "What does my customer need from me right now?" Then decide the method of communication.

The homebuyer's preferred communication method must first be considered. In general, while texting may be preferred by younger homebuyers, older customers are more likely to feel comfortable with a phone call. Older homebuyers may be more likely to prefer emailed information, while texting has eclipsed email as the dominant method for consumers in the 20–35-year-old segment.

However, it's always best not to make assumptions. To best personalize your communication, at contract signing ask homebuyers to identify their preferred communication method (email; text; phone) for resolving (1) non-urgent issues, or (2) questions needing an immediate response. Record these preferences in your CRM or in their permanent file so all other Community Team members can immediately see how best to communicate with each homebuyer.

Home Builder How-To

After our homes start in the field, our Community Team, salespeople, and builder gather every Friday and call every customer together. Some of our Community Teams are very creative with Facetime live shots on site for their out-of-towners, also which is always a welcome touch.

Sometimes we have tough information to share about delays or no appliances, but we have found that regular communication can heal many wounds.

Jacki Matthews, Sales Manager

Good-Better-Best

Are some communication formats more effective than others? Yes! Establishing or strengthening relationships is always a goal for every team member, and this is best accomplished through face-to-face communication. We recognize, however, that this face-to-face option is often impractical. Enter Zoom and FaceTime, fantastic alternatives to an in-person meeting.

The next best option is to have a conversation via phone. Phone calls are a bit less effective but are still more personal than text or email. The only "watch out" with phone conversations is that your construction status update—which could have been a simple *"Hi, your countertops arrived today"*—can easily turn into a 15- to 20-minute conversation on a wide variety of issues. So you'll want to set expectations such as, "Just wanted to call to give you a quick five-minute update on the progress of your home."

Recorded videos offer an ideal format for quickly updating the homebuyer on the status of their home's construction because they are so visual. Stand in front of the home and record a quick selfie with the customer's home in the background. In less than one minute you can produce a simple video that will go a long way toward both updating the customer and enhancing their Emotional Altitude. And, remember, video messages sent via text tend to be viewed more often and more quickly than those sent via email.

Next down the communication hierarchy of effectiveness is text messaging. Most of us open text messages more quickly than emails, and the expectation is that text messages can be very short. Texts are better accepted (if not strongly preferred) by younger homebuyers.

Photos of the home under construction are also easily included in text messages. Without question, photos are the most impactful method for communicating construction progress, particularly for out-of-town buyers who are unable to see their new home very often.

In fact, from within Eliant's *Field Representative App*, sales and construction associates are able to take a photo of the home, click on a standardized message (*"Check out your front door! It's beautiful!"*) and with a single click, send this photo to the selected homebuyer. These photos are very often forwarded to parents, children, and friends and become extremely effective no-cost marketing for your company!

And then there's email. The painful paradox is that email is both the most widely used method of communication and at the same time the least effective. Why is email so ineffective?

- Email equates to noise pollution. An email is competing for attention with hundreds of other messages, most of them spam.

- Email is impersonal. It's very difficult to communicate emotion or excitement in an email.

- Email is one-way. There's no chance for immediate feedback.

- Email makes it almost impossible to gauge the emotions of the customer (other than extreme emotions such as very happy or very angry).

One more word of advice: Change it up! Vary your communication methods throughout the process. Just keep this one guideline in mind: Over-communicating is ALWAYS better than under-communicating.

Home Builder How-To

If a picture is worth a thousand words, what is a video worth? Minimal cost, minimal time, high impact. Using video to keep our customers engaged and informed is not a should; it's a must.

John Christy, Area Sales Manager

Application

- At contract signing, ask homebuyers to identify their preferred form of communication: video conference, text, phone call, and/or email; document each customer's preference.

- Unless the homebuyer selects email as his or her preferred format, avoid emailing status reports.

- Build the weekly communication into the calendar or CRM and also include this on your own schedule. However, avoid setting this up as a formally scheduled event with your customer, with a promised time and day.

- Provide useful information, even if you have no updates to offer. We'll talk more about this in Chapter 10.

- As a bonus, on-site *group* videos can be quickly produced by the Community Team. Simply select a topic of interest to <u>all</u> the homebuyers and homeowners in your community (i.e. status of pool or playground construction) and share it with everyone!

Group Discussion Questions

1. How do you feel about recording personalized videos for your homebuyers? What can you do to make your videos more appealing?

2. What props might you use to enhance a video update? What could you do to make a video relatable to your homebuyer, and increase their Emotional Altitude?

3. When communication is asynchronous (i.e. not sending/receiving at the same time), what do you need to do to ensure the message is interpreted as intended?

4. In what situations would a combination of communication methods be helpful? (e.g. phone call and text)

Chapter Eight

Touring the Home Under Construction

KYLIE AND JANET both completed their home-under-construction tours in the same week. Kylie walked away excited; Janet was nothing but frustrated.

Janet led off the conversation. "This is the point where you tell me how wonderful your tour was and how much you love the people you're working with. Go ahead, get it over with."

"I'm sorry, Janet," replied Kylie. "I take it that your tour didn't go so well."

"To be honest, Matt didn't help things. He was pretty much in the construction superintendent's face the entire time. But he just doesn't trust the builder all that much."

"I can't imagine how Craig would feel if he didn't trust our construction superintendent," said Kylie. "Craig is such a detail freak. But she was really patient and willing to take a long time to answer any questions."

"Is there anything about your entire transaction that isn't going perfectly?" asked Janet

"As a matter of fact, yes," said Kylie. "We really wanted to add a switch so that we can turn on the light to the master bedroom from just outside the bedroom door. It should be a really easy change; they haven't even finished the wiring. They wouldn't do it. Frustrating."

"Why wouldn't they do that?" asked Janet. "Not that we would even bother asking our home builder—we know we'd get their policy thrown back in our faces."

"Our superintendent explained that everything is already set in motion. It's like ordering a new BMW and then deciding you want to change the seat color after the car is already on the assembly line. That one change affects the entire process and introduces quality control issues. That's what the builder said: 'We just won't do anything that could affect the finished quality.' We didn't love the answer, but we understand it."

"Not us," said Janet. "We don't understand what they're doing AND we don't love the process."

"Did you at least enjoy looking at your home being built?" asked Kylie.

"Not really. We were so concerned about having to catch things that they might have missed that we weren't really able to enjoy the process. Not only that, but you could tell that the superintendent just didn't really want to be there. Maybe it's us—I don't know."

"It's not you, Janet. It's just a difficult and trying process."

"Not for you, it's not," said Janet.

Homebuyer Insights

"They could have cleaned up the fast-food wrappers and turned off the blaring music during our frame walk. It took away from the experience."

Insights

What are the goals of a construction walk? There are many:

- Celebrate progress. Customers love to see their home coming together.

- Create confidence (and, correspondingly, trust) in the expertise of the building team.

- Gain clarity and accuracy of the description of the home.

- Elevate the homebuyer's Emotional Altitude.

- Diffuse the homebuyer's anxiety about the process and the people involved.

Customers should conclude the tour with an elevated level of excitement and a deeper level of trust in the builder's care and expertise.

The home-under-construction tour can be a very exciting part of the process for the customer, but it can often lead to confusion and anxiety. How the home-under-construction tour is set up is vital to the success of this part of the process. The Community Team's approach to setting proper expectations is critical.

Prior to the tour, the construction superintendent should ask the salesperson for information about the homebuyer (assuming they have not yet met). What particular things is this homebuyer interested in seeing on this tour? What are the customer's priorities and reasons for purchasing this model? How is the homebuyer planning on using the extra bedrooms? What should be expected by way of personality and demeanor? Have they raised questions or concerns? Are there things to stress (or avoid) during the tour?

Regardless of what information is shared by the salesperson, the construction superintendent should, at the start of the tour, ask key questions of the homebuyer: *"What were your primary reasons for selecting this model? In your mind's eye, what will your favorite space in your new home be?"* (Plan on spending a bit more time in that particular spot during this tour.) These questions—and your customer's responses—will assist in your efforts to make this tour a truly personalized, emotional experience.

Home Builder How-To

We've found that the customers who are most frustrated with the process are the ones who feel like they need to manage the construction of their home. Let us handle the stress of broken windows. This is why you chose us; this is your time to sit back, kick up your feet, and watch the process unfold.

Kaylie Austin, Division Sales Manager

Introducing the Home-Under-Construction Tour

The setup is everything. Customers must have a clear understanding of the WHY of the home tour. It's critically important to set appropriate expectations about the purpose of this tour. Think along the lines of, *"Here is what you'll see; here is what you won't see."*

Some specific points to cover during the introduction:

- Set time expectations (*"This is how much time to plan for this tour."*)

- Preparation that this is an active construction site (*"Construction materials will be viewed during this tour, and it could be a bit messy."*)

- Describe the phase of construction relative to the entire build-cycle (*"Your home is about 60% completed at this point."*)

- Expectation on the change process (*"We will not be able to change anything in the home at this point, no additional customization."*

- Be fully prepared to respond to the #1 likely question: "When will my home be completed?"

Language is Everything

Construction superintendents must be trained on how to adapt their conversations to the preferences of the buyer. Some customers are more savvy; others are neophytes on all things construction-related. Adapt and adjust so as not to talk over or under the customer's level of understanding.

Having said that, the conversation should not be one-sided. Get the homebuyers engaged in the tour, not just as your "audience." Your customers are not there just to listen to you speak. The best tours are those in which the construction superintendent asks many questions and gets the homebuyers engaged.

Many buyers will find it difficult to look at the basic framework of their home and then expand their vision to imagine how the home will look after drywall is installed, paint is applied, carpet is down, etc. Assist them in envisioning the home as it will appear when finished.

In various rooms of the home, ask the homebuyers to imagine how they will place their furniture. Ask about specific life moments around the home and in the yard. Get them to visualize their life in this beautiful new home.

Technical (but not TOO technical)

The home-under-construction tour is an outstanding opportunity to build homebuyer confidence in both the people and the processes. Add concise and relevant information all along the way, but always in bite-sized chunks.

For example, the construction superintendent can take advantage of the opportunity to share his or her background and expertise. They can identify any above-code practices that are in place. They can point to advancements in construction technology that demonstrate why new homes are better, more durable, and safer than older homes.

This is also a great opportunity to support the design center by pointing out the wisdom of some of the customer's choices (*"You'll really enjoy the extra cabinets in the garage. Some of our homeowners have told me how glad they were to add this storage."*)

The home-under-construction tour is a make-or-break moment for many customers. Invest the time it takes to get this right.

Application

- Prior to the home-under-construction tour, be sure to provide the homebuyer with the Lifestyle Bio of the team member conducting the tour.

- Train your construction superintendents in both psychology and language use. This isn't primarily a technical tour; the purpose is to increase the customer's excitement and magnify confidence and trust in the superintendent.

- Make the purpose of the tour clear and definitive *before* the tour begins. Home builders must define a clear process for the tour in writing and train their Community Team members thoroughly. Salespeople should be describing the purpose and process in a manner that is absolutely consistent with what the customer will hear from the team member leading the tour.

- Find ways to increase homebuyer confidence by demonstrating quality and expertise. Brainstorm this with your team. Remember to stay out of the deep weeds.

- End the tour on a positive and upbeat note. Encourage the homebuyer and build up the confidence in their decision.

Group Discussion Questions

1. How should a construction superintendent react if the homebuyer raises a quality concern during the home- under-construction tour?

2. How can a construction superintendent use the tour to relieve worries on the part of the homebuyers?

3. What are some ways to complete a home-under-construction tour on a high note?

Chapter Nine

Delivering Bad News

KYLIE AND CRAIG were none too pleased with the news. The two-week delay in their move-in date would cause them to scramble in adjusting their plans. All this over an unexpected shortage of drywall throughout the region. The double whammy occurred when they were informed of a change in their shower tile selection.

Craig and Kylie double-teamed the superintendent with their concerns.

"Drywall is a pretty basic and important component," complained Craig. "I don't know how this couldn't have been planned for."

"And the shower tile we chose for the guest bathroom is now unavailable. So we have to make a trade-off to our second choice. I know it's just the guest bathroom, but I loved that tile!"

The Matchless Homes construction superintendent replied, "I get it. I know this is frustrating. We're still working on other solutions for the drywall. But you must understand that the entire region is dealing with the same issue. One of the major suppliers went out of business unexpectedly and everything is being bought up. As for the tile, this is why we had that initial conversation several weeks ago about the inevitable problem with discontinuations. Sometimes we're simply at the mercy of our suppliers. I'm glad you were able to make a new selection, even if it was your second favorite."

Craig asked if there was any chance they could still make the original schedule; he was loath to change his moving plans. The response: "It will be in your best interest to assume a delay. Otherwise you'll get to the closing and have nowhere to go."

The Community Team was adamant and also empathetic. They apologized for the delay even though it was out of their control. They assured Kylie and Craig that they were doing all they could to solve the problem.

The situation was identical at Connor Gregory Homes, but the delivery of that message to Janet and Matt was far different. The salesperson—not the construction superintendent—called the couple and said that the purchasing department was looking at a different supplier and, if they came through, they would be able to stay with the original schedule.

Janet was encouraged to be hopeful that the target date would still be met, and she made no plans to alter her moving schedule. Matt was the one who suggested that it might be time to rethink the moving schedule, but Janet took comfort in the confidence of the salesperson.

On their Saturday morning walk, Janet took the opportunity to press Kylie with some good-natured gloating.

"Looks like things are going our way for once, and your perfect experience has come to an end!"

"Don't be too sure yet," replied Kylie. "There's still plenty that could go right or wrong…for both of us."

"Well, as long as we close on time, we'll be fine. If not, somebody's gonna pay and it won't be pretty."

Homebuyer Insights

"Things go wrong—we get that. But why weren't we told? Why did we have to discover the problems? And what else were they hiding from us? We couldn't make any plans because we didn't know what we had not yet been told."

Insights

No transaction is perfect; thus the skill set of delivering bad news must be trained thoroughly and practiced to perfection via role playing. Of course, this is the type of situation that most Community Team members find uncomfortable. The desire to practice an appropriate response ahead of time does not come naturally; most people dislike the very idea of practicing and, especially, role playing.

Customer-centered home builders will dedicate the time to train and deal with the discomfort of role playing to prepare for such difficult situations. Ultimately, homebuyers are the beneficiaries of this training and practice. Since problems are inevitable in the process, this skillset is a non-negotiable aspect of providing a great experience.

The Inevitability of Bad News

No transaction is perfect; thus *there will always be bad news to share.* Expect this to occur with every homebuyer and prepare for it in advance. It should not come as a surprise when things head a bit south.

Tie the delivery of bad news into previous expectation-setting conversations. If the Community Team has done its job properly, the conversation should begin with something like, "Remember when I said that…?" This is where the expectation-setting discussion will really pay off. If you haven't warned a customer of the inevitability of delays, product shortages, mistakes, etc., you'll find your customers frustrated and, often, angry.

The Bad News Mindset

Community Team members want to provide great service. They are often pleasers, and they want their customers to always feel happy about the process. But this mindset can be dangerous. When painting too rosy a picture, you often set up for failure.

Set proper expectations. Learn what to say, and what NOT to say. In each of your departmental meetings, rehearse and role play the way you'll share bad news about one negative event (e.g., error in loan docs; delay in completing the driveway cement; vandalism on the property).

But you can also adjust your perspective about delivering bad news. This is an opportunity to show how professional you are, and how good you are in improving your service level to overcome the bad news. Sure, it's hard, but you're a professional—accept this as a challenge!

Home Builder How-To

Bad news is inevitable in the building journey; the key is the medium and timing of bad news. Always focus on delivering the news in person or on the telephone, following up with details in writing. And remember, delivery is everything! It's not what you say—it's HOW you say it.

Kathryn Catherwood, Director of Sales and Marketing

10 Steps for Sharing Bad News

1. **No surprises**. From the beginning of your relationship with the customer, set the expectation that during the next few months things are likely to happen to delay the construction, design, or loan process. Soften the blow where you can. If you can see the problem or delay coming, give the customer a warning that there may be a problem on the horizon.

   Example: *"Mr. Johnson, just letting you know that our purchasing team has alerted me that the shortage and delays in getting cabinets will probably begin impacting our construction schedule next month. Although we're actively searching for alternative suppliers, we may be delayed in finishing your cabinets. I'll continue updating you as I learn more information."*

2. **Collect all the facts** before sharing the bad news with your customer. Speak personally to a field representative who has current first-hand knowledge about this issue.

3. **Never delay delivering bad news**. The situation is unlikely to get better. Your speech won't get any easier! The worst-case scenario is for your customer to discover the problem before you tell him. When delivering bad news, treat each customer as if he or she is your best friend. How would you communicate bad news if this were your best friend (or your mom)? Would you be less likely to delay?

4. **Total transparency and honesty**: Share everything; don't hold back. Your customer needs the whole story. Your candor will earn your customer's respect. Never blame the customer or throw one of your teammates under the bus—even if the delay (or any problem) was their fault!

5. **Apologize**: You represent your company. Even if you did not create or cause the problem, you must sincerely apologize on behalf of the company.

6. **Show authentic empathy**. Put yourself in your customer's shoes and imagine how he or she feels. *"You must be extremely frustrated with this delay."* Don't try to minimize the situation with statements like, *"It could have been worse,"* or insincere statements like,

"I know how you feel." With all due respect, how can you possibly relate to this family's situation? Your homebuyer's family of five is living in a motel waiting for their home to be completed. They are racking up expenses they had not budgeted for. All they get are six channels on their room's TV, one of which is the *"Olympic Curling Network."* Their furniture was placed in storage. Their family Thanksgiving dinner was at Waffle House. You DON'T know how they feel! Acknowledge that.

7. **Consider the communication format**. Face-to-face or phone communication is best. This allows you to gauge and respond to the customer's reaction. When sharing bad news, text or email messages should be avoided and voicemail should only be used as a means of last resort.

8. **Offer a solution.** Describe possible solutions and take responsibility for resolving the issue, but do *not* make promises you aren't prepared to *beat* 95% of the time.

9. **Follow up to confirm the problem was corrected.** Send a note to again apologize and express empathy with what the customer had to face.

10. **Add value.** Reach into your bag of tricks and pull out a "surprise and delight" opportunity, some kind of unexpected value-add that will ease some of the pain brought on by the bad news.

There will always be bad news to share. Expect this to occur with every buyer. Prepare for it. Set proper expectations. Learn what to say, what NOT to say, and train and practice rigorously with your Community Teams.

Application

- Deliver bad news as a team when possible. Yes, this adds complication on your side of things, but it means the world to the homebuyer and tends to reduce emotion levels.

- Script out your bad news messages and practice repeatedly *before* contacting the homebuyer. There is a right way to deliver bad news. Don't wait for your Community Team members to just make it up on the fly.

- Commit to a "we" approach for the entire team. No blaming. We win together and we struggle together, but blaming a different department does nothing but aggravate the customer and erode trust.

Group Discussion Questions

1. What is the worst bad news you've had to deliver to a homebuyer? What went well? What didn't?

2. What are the benefits of using a sandwich approach (good news, bad news, good news) to deliver bad news to the homebuyer? How could this approach backfire?

3. How would you respond to specific customer reactions to bad news? (e.g. tears, anger, disbelief, threats of legal action)

4. What would happen if you openly blamed a member of the Community Team for a snafu that caused customer issues?

Chapter Ten

The Planned Surprise Strategy

ON THEIR SATURDAY MORNING WALK, Kylie updated Janet on the amazing dinner they'd enjoyed the evening before.

"So, Craig's boss treated us to a very high-end meal at Localis, his favorite restaurant in Midtown. First-class all the way, Michelin star, tasting menu, the whole nine yards. It was incredible."

"Sounds awesome," said Janet. "What was your favorite part?"

Kylie paused to reflect on the experience. "I guess it was the extras. The food was fantastic—the best meal I've ever had. But it was the glass of champagne when we told them it was a celebration of our new home. It was the chef taking the time to tell us his inspiration behind the dishes. The extra piece of octopus they gave to Craig because he raved about it so much. It was just a number of small but very cool touches that we never expected."

"That sounds incredible," replied Janet. "It sounds like your home builder and the restaurant owner both went to the same school."

"Funny you should mention that," said Kylie. "Because this very morning we received a stack of these cool moving box labels from our home builder. We can write down what's in the box and which room it goes to, and the labels have cute little sayings and quotes about homes. It was just a fun little surprise."

"You and Craig really made a good choice. I'm sure we'll love our home once we're in it, but right now we just feel like we're invisible. I have to call the salesperson for updates because I'm pretty sure he wouldn't call me otherwise. And talking to anyone else in the company? Forget it."

"There might still be time for you to jump ship and join me over at Matchless Homes," suggested Kylie.

"We'll hang in there for a bit longer," replied Janet. "Maybe they'll surprise us and send us a pack of gum."

"Fingers crossed!"

Insights

Every customer loosely monitors a kind of "bank account" of experiences throughout the process. Good experiences provided by the home builder are deposits into the account; bad experiences are withdrawals. The objective for the home builder is to never be overdrawn.

This requires an intentional effort on behalf of the entire team to seek out deposit opportunities. But it also requires a strategic and systematic process for doing so. There is an intentionality to this concept that is simple to grasp but too often ignored. This is an opportunity for a huge payoff with relatively minimal efforts.

We call this the "Planned Surprise" strategy, a process based upon a remarkably simple premise:

> *If you do what your customers expect,*
> *you get satisfied homebuyers. When you*
> *surprise your customers with unexpected*
> *experiences, you get delighted homebuyers.*

Let's break that down.

Homebuyer Insights

"We received a nice letter from the principal of the elementary school where our kids would attend. She welcomed us to the neighborhood and encouraged us to ask any questions we might have. It was great of the builder to set that up."

Satisfied vs. Delighted

When you simply meet your promises and commitments, you get satisfied homebuyers. But since satisfied customers neither passionately nor proactively refer their friends to you, the end goal must go beyond customer satisfaction. The end goal is to create frequent, passionate referrals from your homebuyers and homeowners.

Think about that for a moment. Passion is an absolutely essential element of a referral. When was the last time you received a passionate endorsement of an excellent tuna sandwich? Or a really good pencil? People generally aren't passionate about such things, so they don't offer referrals. The presence of passion drives referrals, both positive and negative.

To help reach this goal, you must look for ways to delight homebuyers by doing small but unexpected extras that take them by surprise, things that deliver just a bit more than they expected from their salesperson, builder, lender, design studio, or warranty rep. You must consistently perform in a manner that compels homebuyers to tell their friends, *"I never expected my home builder to…"*

You can finish that sentence in any number of ways:

- *"I never expected my home builder to remind me of the AYSO soccer sign-ups."*

- *"I never expected my home builder to arrange a Zoom call with the local internet provider."*

- *"I never expected my home builder to deliver pizza on our move-in day."*

- *"I never expected my home builder to pick up our used boxes after we unpacked."*

A one-degree rise in the temperature of water from 211 to 212 degrees can drive a locomotive. In the same way, small, inexpensive but unexpected events or gifts are disproportionately powerful and can be used to create *delighted* customers.

Home Builder How-To

During the sales process, the Sales Consultant got to know the young son of the buyers. He was at every appointment and always had his Superman toy with him.

During the demonstration phase, he selected his room and couldn't wait to enjoy it. During their walk through before closing, the buyers were floored when they walked into that room and saw that the Sales Consultant had purchased Superman wall vinyls and used them to decorate the room.

That little boy screamed in delight and beamed with pride announcing that his room was already ready for him. A few dollars and a big heart and that Sales Consultant made a truly magical memory for that buyer.

Jaymie Catalano Dimbath,
Vice President of Sales and Marketing

Planned Surprises Examples

Most of our clients' Planned Surprises are low-cost or no-cost items:

- A photo at contract signing

- E-mailed school schedules

- Little League sign-up alerts

- A list of community events coming up in the next six months

- Emailed tips to help make the home-packing process more efficient

- Custom home builder key chains

- Builder-branded packing-box labels

- Introductions to backyard landscape companies

- An interior design magazine

These small events may come as a surprise to your customers, but they should be *planned* by your team for a systematic delivery process to every homebuyer. Don't leave this activity to chance or last-minute impulse.

In 2008, Eliant created *"The Planned Surprise Strategy"* and began including this powerful concept in their Customer Experience Certification programs. As a result, builders and lenders utilizing Planned Surprises demonstrated significant increases in homebuyers' willingness to recommend them to a friend.

The strength of this process is found in the systematic delivery of a planned series of low-cost or no-cost surprise events at some of the key milestones during the purchase and move-in experience.

Key milestones could include:

- Contract signing

- First meeting with loan officer

- First meeting with design studio designer

- Loan approval

- Final design studio sign-off

- Final orientation walk-through

- Move-in day

- First customer service visit to home

- 6-month anniversary of move-in

- 1-year anniversary

- 2-year anniversary

IMPORTANT: The key is to deliver these Planned Surprises AS A SURPRISE! Never promise or allude to these surprises. Remind sales associates that they should not mention these planned surprises to prospective homebuyers as a means of "bragging" about the home builder's commitment to delighting their customers. The surprise is the required element to the success of this process. If customers know what's coming, they will receive what they are now expecting, and this only creates satisfaction, not delight!

Application

- Get the team involved. They will likely thoroughly enjoy coming up with surprise and delight opportunities. Find a "Surprise and Delight Czar" and let that person drive the initiative company-wide.

- Plan once; repeat often. Make sure your surprises are easily repeatable and understood by all team members.

- Determine and favor opportunities that are "disproportionately powerful": High in impact but relatively low in effort. You might need to brainstorm several different possible options, and then settle in on the high-impact/low-effort choices.

- Have other such surprise and delight practices "in the bag" in the event of problems with a particular home or customer.

Group Discussion Questions

1. Who from your Community Team would make the best Surprise and Delight Czar? How can you keep him or her feeling motivated and supported in this role?

2. What are the two or three most critical events in the customer journey that you will want to celebrate with a Planned Surprise item?

3. Should you use different Planned Surprise items for different customers?

4. Who from your Community Team should deliver your Planned Surprise items?

SECTION 3:

The Crucial 60 Days

Chapter Eleven

Setting Expectations for the Final Stretch

"ARE YOU NERVOUS, KYLIE?" asked Janet on their Saturday morning walk. "We're getting close now."

"I wouldn't say nervous," Kylie replied. "Excited for sure. But everything is going according to plan so far. What the home builder has told us is pretty much exactly what has happened. How are you feeling?"

"We'd feel much better if we had an actual person to talk to."

"What does that mean?" asked Kylie.

"We just got an email from our home builder. They moved our salesperson to a different community and now someone new is taking over. The email went on and on and about how this will be a seamless transition, blah, blah, whatever. But nothing has been seamless so far, so Matt and I are even more concerned."

"Maybe the new salesperson will be better about keeping you informed."

"Right," said Janet with a sneer. "I called the new salesperson and she said—I quote—'We're just trying to deal with the people who are moving in next week. I'll call you after that and give you an update.' She wasn't rude about it, but it's really clear that she's in over her head."

"What are you going to do?" asked Kylie.

"I found the name of the sales manager for the company and I've left two messages; no response yet. In the meantime, we'll just double-down on asking questions and basically bothering them until we get answers. Matt is already visiting the site almost every day. If I have to stop by the sales office every day, so be it."

"I'm so sorry," said Kylie. "Sounds rough."

Janet replied, "And I can't even keep track of all the things I need to do to prepare for the move."

"I can help you with that," said Kylie. "Our salesperson gave us a very detailed 'what to expect' checklist, as well as a list of things that we should be doing each week between now and the move-in date."

"I would love to get a copy of that. It will answer a lot of questions."

"Sure thing," said Kylie.

"And maybe you can persuade *your* Community Team to talk to *my* Community Team about how to do this job right!"

"I'll see what I can do about that," Janet said with a knowing laugh.

Insights

As homebuyers close in on their move-in date, life becomes increasingly anxious and complex. The check-list of things-to-do gets longer and longer, while the days seem to get shorter and shorter. Too little time, too many tasks.

The daunting prospect of packing all their belongings, emptying their storage unit, and moving out of their current residence is enough to make some buyers question whether they should be hiring a mover or a psychiatrist.

The best home builders help their customers by patiently walking through all the steps and offering suggestions on how to best navigate the process. Since most homebuyers don't expect this kind of active service and support from their home builder, this is truly an "extra-credit" activity that will impact the buyer's willingness to recommend the builder to a friend.

Think: "surprise and delight" opportunity.

These steps include (but are certainly not limited to):

- Setting *realistic* expectations for the likelihood of possible delays

- Offering packing tips and branded box labels

- Providing a list of utility transition websites, email addresses, and phone numbers

- Providing the names and locations of local storage options

- Sending a list of local consignment shops for furniture sale or purchase (perhaps with a discount coupon arranged by the builder)

- Setting the final walk-through expectations and scheduling

This process can be communicated by means of a thorough "What to Expect" checklist for the customer.

Bottom line: Get creative. Think like a homebuyer. What would you need?

Homebuyer Insights

"We were handed a "map" that walked us through what would happen in the last thirty days. We've never purchased a home before, so it was great information and very helpful."

The Communication Pattern

Communication must increase as the completion date draws near. The one-call-per-week cadence that was appropriate in the beginning is now insufficient. As the closing date approaches, the amount of proactive communication with tips and construction status should increase.

This is especially important in special cases:

- With first-time homebuyers who are unfamiliar with the process

- With buyers who appear to be unusually anxious about their move

- With buyers who have frequently complained about the purchase process

The more that can be communicated in writing, the easier it is for the customer to grasp. Salespeople must continue to raise the customer's Emotional Altitude as the closing date draws near.

Dealing with Homebuyer Anxiety

Anxiety is the death of homebuyer referrals. As the stakes are continually raised during the pre-move-in period, homebuyers' worst-case fears come floating to the surface. This creates an extra level of angst which in turn can quickly transform an acquiescent buyer into an aggressive belligerent.

What are some typical buyer fears?

- *The close will be delayed or postponed because…*

- *The construction of the home will not be completed on the promised date.*

- *I will become unhappy with a home-quality issue during the final walk and refuse to close.*

- *There will be a last-minute issue with my loan.*

- *Loan docs will not be delivered to the escrow office in time.*

- *There will be errors in my docs which cannot be quickly corrected.*

- *The weather on my projected move-in day is expected to be snowing/raining/too cold/too hot.*

- *What will we do with our dogs/cats/llamas during the move?*

- *Will the moving van arrive on time?*

- *What if some furniture is damaged during the move?*

- *Since I have already sold my home, I will have no place to stay.*

That list is not exhaustive; we've just scratched the surface. Even small glitches in the process can trigger negative reactions from your anxious buyer.

Keep in mind that first-time homebuyers are often so unaware of the potential problems that they don't worry about many of these possible errors and omissions. But experienced homeowners have been through this before, and consequently, their anxiety level can often be even higher than entry-level homebuyers.

You can earn trust throughout the purchase process by doing unexpected things to help the homebuyer and also by making promises you intend to *beat* (and by that we mean beat 95% of the time!) When homebuyers trust you, delays and errors are more likely to be tolerated or even ignored.

Continue being honest, totally transparent, and proactive with communication about delays in the delivery of materials or changes in the schedule.

Home Builder How-To

There's so much that goes on in the final weeks of construction. Remind people that ahead of time. We get to write chaotic stories with happy endings. While it may look chaotic, that's to be expected. Continue to remind people of what's to come at the end.

Kathryn Catherwood, Director of Sales and Marketing

Application

- Nothing beats complete and frequent communication. Community Teams should have a communication pattern built into their systems, and that pattern should set the standard for communication frequency. That frequency must *increase* the closer the buyer gets to the move-in date.

- The more demanding the customer, the more important it is to initiate proactive communication, even on a daily basis if necessary. Consider developing a "FAB" (for anxious buyers) process. What are some ways to ramp up the service when you know a customer is particularly concerned?

- .Community Teams must be aware that stress levels rise as homebuyers draw closer to the moving day. Boosting the Emotional Altitude then becomes the order of the day. Internal pep talks go a long way toward displaying that positive energy to the customer.

Group Discussion Questions

1. Murphy's Law says "Whatever can go wrong, will go wrong." But there's a corollary: "Whatever CAN'T go wrong, won't go wrong." Think of some of the most common problems that happen during the final stretch and discuss ways to mistake-proof or prevent them from happening at all.

2. How might the management of final-stretch events impact customer satisfaction and the likelihood of a referral?

3. How does focusing on customer nervousness during the final stretch help Community Team members manage their own anxieties?

4. Let's have a bit of comic relief. What are some of the strangest and funniest things that have happened during the final stretch? How did you deal with these unexpected surprises?

Chapter Twelve

Communicating Move-In Dates

KYLIE CALLED JANET to give her the good news.

"It's happening!" she said. "We just talked to our home builder and they told us that we're now six weeks away from move-in, and that it's time to start packing. I'm really excited."

"Good for you, Kylie," Janet replied. "I hope that works out for you. We're supposed to be four weeks out but our new salesperson is suddenly really reluctant to give us a date. I have to give notice to our landlord, but I don't know when to do that."

"What did your salesperson say?" asked Kylie.

"Well," replied Janet, "She didn't *say* anything. She sent us an email saying—and I quote—"We should be good to go.""

"I take it you're not confident that your home will be ready in four weeks?" asked Kylie. "What does your construction superintendent say?"

"Is that a joke, Kylie? We talked to one construction guy back during our frame walk, and that guy has been moved out to another job."

"You should probably hold off on giving your landlord any notice. Too many things can go wrong."

"We might be moving in with you if the timing doesn't work out, Kylie!"

Homebuyer Insights

"To wait until FIVE DAYS before move-in to give us an actual moving date was infuriating. It made our planning impossible."

Insights

Question: When does move-in expectation management begin? Answer: at (or even before) contract signing, when buyers ask the most important question: *"When will I be able to move my family in?"*

For the best home builders, the conversation surrounding move-in dates is an ongoing and consistent dialogue. This begins with setting the right expectations at contract signing and continues throughout the construction process. The home stretch conversation should begin with the words, "As we have been saying all along..."

This explanation can be supplemented with third-party stories, both of customers who padded their schedule (and had a much more enjoyable transaction) and then those who tried to time the move to a specific date (and ended up frustrated and massively inconvenienced).

Home Builder How-To

Prospective buyers and buyers at contract *always* ask about their closing date. In response, our sales associates don't start with a "window," but do present an "estimated" close date. Sales associates are trained to discuss all the moving parts, materials, and workers involved in completing their home and reinforce that it is not an easily predictable process, and that there will likely be updates or changes to the estimated close date.

We provide buyers a "Weekly Community Update" with ongoing construction progress and any changes to their estimated move-in date. The word "estimated" is consistently used when referring to any dates:

- *We're estimating Phase 1 closings to begin January 29.*
- *We monitor our schedules each week and will keep you updated with any changes.*

Our goal is to communicate status proactively, so our buyers don't ever feel a need to call and ask. In fact, our *Eliant* customer experience surveys show a 99.7% rating for our construction status communication, #1 ranked of Eliant's 200+ clients!

We let buyers know that we'll have a "firm" close date approximately 30 days out—with the usual caveat that there could still be changes if something unexpected happens. We also remind buyers to keep two weeks of overlap on their current residence if possible.

Brian Taylor, Senior Director of Sales

The Overly Optimistic Salesperson

It's in the nature of salespeople to be optimistic, but this is where providing too rosy a picture is potentially disastrous. The consequences of getting this wrong are just too severe. The conservative approach is best.

To take the guesswork out of the occasion (and to guard against irrational optimism on behalf of the salesperson), the move-in date conversation should be well-rehearsed and approved by the leadership team. Never were the words "under-promise and over-deliver" more important.

From the Customer's Perspective

One of the grandest, most memorable events in your customers' lives is the day they move into their new home. As their excitement (and anxiety) builds prior to the purchase decision, they are already imagining the move-in experience, setting up their furniture, and watching their kids' joyful response.

With this anxiety in mind, the homebuyer's most important question (*"When will I be able to move my family"*) is a 100% predictable event in the life of every new home salesperson. In fact, it will typically be asked on multiple occasions. Count on being asked one—or more—times before the buyer makes a purchase decision, and then again at the time of contract signing.

Therefore, it's imperative for the home builder to set a structured sequence for proactively communicating the estimated move-in date. Salespeople must be totally prepared (and formally trained with role-playing practice) to respond to this important question and must respond the same way each time.

To make it easier for the salesperson and homebuyer, and to reduce the number of times the customer feels it necessary to ask this question, the "Estimated Closing Date Communication Schedule" should be shared with the buyer *in writing* at contract signing. Presenting this written document to the buyer makes it more "official," demonstrates the professionalism of the builder, helps reduce the buyer's anxiety, and builds the homebuyer's trust and confidence in the builder, i.e., *"They've clearly done this before."*

Explaining the Process of Setting Move-In Dates

The "Estimated Closing Date Communication Schedule" is a list of construction milestones that trigger a proactive communication of the updated estimated date. The selection of these milestone-trigger events (like trenching; drywall; cabinet installation) must be determined in a discussion between sales and construction superintendents. Salespeople, design center consultants, superintendents, and loan and escrow officers should then have access to this electronic document so they can all consistently respond to the homebuyer's question.

At contract, this document should be presented to the homebuyer, with a wide-ranging estimated closing date range at the top of the page (e.g., "October to December"). Although the milestone triggers in the "Estimated Closing Date Schedule" will differ from home builder to home builder, the important point is to have a schedule to guide your communication. Here's one conservative example that provides a large degree of flexibility to the builder:

- At contract, give a three-month window: *"We will finish your home between October and December."*

- At trenching (or another selected milestone) give a two-month window: *"We will finish your home between November and December."*

- At framing, give a six-week window: *"We will finish your home between October 15 and December 1."*

- At completion of drywall, give a four- to five-week window: *"We will finish your home between October 20 and November 29."*

- After cabinet installation, give a ten-day window: *"We will finish your home between November 12 and 22."*

- At four to five weeks prior to the estimated close of escrow date, give a specific date: *"You will be able to move into your home on November 21."*

Here's another way to share this information: About eight to ten weeks in advance of the anticipated completion or closing date of the home, the home builder should provide the homebuyer with the targeted _week_ of the home's completion and closing.

Then, five to six weeks before the anticipated close date, the homebuyer should be given a <u>*specific date*</u> of the projected closing. This advance notice should allow the soon-to-be homeowner sufficient time to schedule a mover.

Keep in mind that during periods of heavy move-outs across the country (e.g., June, July, August), arranging for a mover requires a longer lead time, so two to three weeks must be added to the numbers given above.

Application

- This expectation-setting conversation requires a company-wide strategy. In setting this strategy, keep in mind a very specific parameter: Do not make a promise that you cannot keep or beat!

- With the strategy in place, training must follow. This detailed training must include multiple practice sessions and role playing for delivering the move-in message. These sessions should be placed on video for future training of new team members.

- Consider holding a homebuyer panel so that Community Team members can better understand the customer's journey and how move-in dates have an emotional effect on the customer. Bring in five to six homebuyers who are willing to be honest about their experience. Select a moderator who will ask the questions. Invite everyone in the company or division to sit in. The perspective of someone who's going through the process is invaluable. (Pro Tip: Find people who are neutrally satisfied—not delighted and not upset. This is where the best learning opportunities come from.)

Group Discussion Questions

1. Why is it important to accompany any communication of move-in date with written follow-up?

2. Move-in day can drive homeowner emotions from deep lows to never-before-experienced highs. Why is it important that move-in communications not cause negative emotions?

3. Brainstorm 10 negative consequences the homebuyer might have to deal with if the move-in date is pushed back.

4. Within your organization, what is the best way to make sure the homebuyer has the most up-to-date information on projected move-in date at all times?

Chapter Thirteen

The Homeowner Orientation Tour

KYLIE AND CRAIG HAD A GREAT TIME touring their new home. The home wasn't exactly perfect; a few things were pointed out to them and a plan to fix those items was put in place, along with expected completion dates for each entry.

Craig requested that some of the wall texture be redone but was told by the customer care representative that the way the wall was finished was consistent with the quality of the model home, the standard used to determine quality levels. Craig wasn't thrilled, but he understood.

At the end of the tour, Kylie and Craig were handed a photo album of their home, from foundation to completion. And much to their surprise, the president of Matchless Homes came by to offer her congratulations.

Janet and Matt, meanwhile, had an entirely different experience. After their completion date was delayed with poor communication from the builder, Matt came into the tour—having been warned by a friend that the home builder would miss a lot of details—with a rip-it-apart mindset. The conversations were tense and unpleasant.

Janet kept count of the number of times the word "policy" was used by the superintendent: thirteen, to be precise. The superintendent begrudgingly gave in on some concerns but dug in his heels on relative minor fixes elsewhere.

At the very end of the tour, Janet and Matt were told that there was one key issue: The home had no gas meter. The supplier had run short and the estimated time of delivery would be two weeks.

Matt was furious! They were packed up and ready to go, and they could not stay in their old home. They had already arranged for a moving crew, child care, and time off of work. The salesperson felt bad, but Janet was left with the impression that this was not the first time something like this had happened.

While Kylie and Craig were in the process of moving in, Janet and Matt were scrambling to find a place to live.

Homebuyer Insights

"Nobody showed up for the final walk. I texted him. He said he was at the gym and would not get to work until 10 a.m."

Insights

The first critical step is to define what the homeowner orientation tour is…and what it is not. Taking a "tear this home apart" approach is beneficial neither to the home builder nor the customer. Too often, the setting of this particular stage is flawed and the results are correspondingly bad.

Our most successful home builder clients consider this to be an "Orientation Tour" (sometimes labeled a "Welcome Home Tour"), not a walk-through. The purpose of the event is three-fold:

1. Demonstrate the operation of key features

2. Show off the craftsmanship with pride to the new homeowner

3. Celebrate the customer's big day and their beautiful new home

We believe that the Orientation Tour is primarily about how to enjoy the home for years to come. The vibe should be celebratory. The enthusiasm—both of the home builder and the homebuyer—should be palpable.

Homebuyer Insights

"Joke is on us!! They basically went around the house and just peeled off (the blue tape) and checked it off!!!"

What the Orientation Tour is NOT

The last thing the home builder wants is to turn this Orientation Tour into a defect hunt. This is not a "blue-tape" event, where buyers are allowed to point out every tiny perceived flaw in wall texture and other features. This will lead to nothing but trouble.

Furthermore, this should not be targeted as a "Zero-item Walk-Through," as some home builders claim to aim for. In many cases, employees are rewarded for reporting fewer items on their punch lists. Of course, this easily leads to an underreporting of issues that are important to homebuyers.

Customers observe and take note of this practice and they report it in their Eliant evaluations. Consequently, they lose trust in their home builder, particularly in the construction superintendent.

Even worse, this kind of bonus system makes it more likely that superintendents will "double-list" during the tour. There is one list of *all* the items and another that becomes the official (and very short) punch list turned into the company after being signed off by the homebuyer. In these circumstances, the customer is told not to worry—all the items will be taken care of! Hardly a model of customer-centric practice.

Homebuyer Insights

"My walk-through was an overwhelming experience in a good way. I was prepared with my lists and so was my builder. He was courteous and patient with me during this process."

Who Should Conduct the Orientation Tour?

We believe the best practice is that the construction super-intendent should *not* be the one to conduct the Orientation Tour, rather that it should be led by someone in the customer care or warranty department. In this way, an honest punch list is created during the tour and the responsibility for resolving the items on this list is then handed back to the superintendent to correct those things which should have been completed prior to the tour.

Homebuyer Insights

"I liked the "how to" explanations of the technology and systems in the home. I appreciated not having to figure out everything on our own."

What Promises Should be Made?

The customer's main concern is this: *When* will items be corrected. Accordingly, this should not be left to guess. This is certainly not the time to be overly optimistic. In fact, this is a "surprise and delight" opportunity.

Here is a rough guideline to help determine the timelines to be communicated:

- Promise 30 days if you firmly believe the list will be cleared in <15 days

- Promise 45 days if you firmly believe the list will be cleared in <30 days

- Promise 60 days if you firmly believe the list will be cleared in <45 days

Always plan to *beat* your promises. Homebuyers will be annoyed, and often angry, if their punch list items are not quickly resolved. They believe that these items should have been completed BEFORE move-in, not after. Imagine that!

Home Builder How-To

The customer hired us to build a quality home. The home must be 100% complete for the Home Orientation walk. The walk is not for the customer to help find items that need to be fixed.

John Upchurch, Vice President of Sales and Marketing

Application

- Get your Community Teams involved in both crafting and perfecting the introduction of the Orientation Tour. Make sure everyone is on the same page with how the tour will be introduced.

- All employees, regardless of department, should regularly attend homebuyer orientation tours. This is a fantastic way to interact with actual customers, and it offers a wonderful appreciation both for the homes that are built and the impact on people's lives.

- Set up regular practice sessions and include role-playing on how to handle difficult and particularly picky customers. Practice the art of saying "no."

Group Discussion Questions

1. Why is it a good idea to have written information on key features and operations to give to customers on this busy day?

2. How is the Orientation Tour different from a walk-through to create a punch list?

3. Why is it good to have someone other than the construction superintendent lead the Orientation Tour?

4. How does the approach of doing an "Orientation Tour" help maintain a homebuyer's Emotional Altitude?

Chapter Fourteen

From Homebuyer to Homeowner

JANET SAT IN THE KITCHEN of her in-laws' home checking her Instagram feed. Up popped a post from Kylie, a video that the Matchless Homes salesperson had posted of their Key Ceremony. Janet saw Kylie and Craig smiling warmly as congratulations were offered all around.

Janet called Kylie an hour later.

"Well, I guess my misery is complete."

"What are you talking about?" asked Kylie.

"I saw your Instagram post. A Key Ceremony? Really?"

"Yeah, sorry about that. I didn't want you to feel bad," replied Kylie.

"What was that they handed you?" asked Janet. "It looked like a small jewelry box."

"It was, actually. The key sat there in the box on a piece of velvet. It felt like someone was proposing to us. I have to admit; it made the moment really special."

"I'm happy for you—really, I am. When can I see the place?"

"We aren't moving officially for a couple of days; we want to take our time. But I'm heading over again in about an hour," replied Kylie. "Want to stop by?"

"I have nothing else to do," said Janet. "Other than to take up space in someone else's house. I'm going stir crazy."

"I put the coffee pot in the last box. I'll bring it and you can help me break in the new kitchen."

Homebuyer Insights

"The moment we were handed the keys—with the builder, our warranty rep, the vice president, and the salesperson all there—we felt really special. Thank you!"

Insights

Becoming a homeowner is a momentous occasion in anyone's life. Too many home builders miss the opportunity to understand, appreciate, and respond to the significance of this moment. The best companies take a customer-centric view on what is really happening here.

The transition from homebuyer to homeowner should be celebratory by design. It doesn't have to be elaborate or costly or time-consuming. It just needs to be memorable. It's the unexpected nature of the celebration that is the critical element.

Someone on the team needs to take the lead to coordinate the celebration, likely the salesperson. And the entire

Community Team should participate so that they can enjoy this part of the process as much as the homebuyer does. It's what makes all the hard work and difficult moments worthwhile!

The Moment

The best practice to initiate here could be labeled as the Key Ceremony. This is *not* something that should be promised to the buyer in advance; rather it should be another "surprise and delight" opportunity.

Ideally, all members of the Community Team attend the Key Ceremony. This is, of course, not feasible at times, but is certainly a suggested best practice.

This moment represents the culmination of the buyer's dream, and a lot of work by many people (builder, buyer, lender, escrow, etc.) to get to this point.

Homebuyer Insights

"Was a very special moment! The bow on the door and gift bag and our builder meeting us there...It felt like a very warm homecoming."

Examples

Here are several different ideas for executing an effective and memorable Key Ceremony:

- Take a photo of the homebuyer(s) holding up the key to their new home. This is particularly effective if they are standing in front of the community signage. Taking a picture in front of their completed home also works.

- This photo can be emailed to the homebuyer; it will undoubtedly be forwarded to all of their friends and relatives. (Giving you free marketing!)

- To make this moment even more unforgettable, print the photo immediately and place it in an inexpensive frame to hand to the buyer along with the keys— another lifetime memory!

- A key holder is also a nice touch, perhaps delivered in a decorative box that is opened like the revealing of an engagement ring.

- A gigantic bow on the front or garage door makes the moment special, and it can be collected and reused for other homes as they are completed.

- Let the nearby neighbors know that new people are moving in.

- A wonderful Planned Surprise is to offer complimentary pick-up of their packing boxes in 10 to 14 days. (As an added bonus to the branded packing labels provided by the builder that was discussed in

Chapter Four, the boxes picked up from one new owner can be offered to someone who will be moving in soon.)

Home Builder How-To

"I live for the moment we deliver the keys. I have an entire photo album showing pictures of me with clients when they receive their keys. It's a special moment for them… and for me!"

Kiera Saunders, Sales Representative

Application

- Form a committee who will brainstorm ideas for a perfect surprise and delight opportunity at the time of move-in. Make sure it is easily repeatable.

- Consider having other company employees attend the ceremony when the keys are handed over. So many people in the main office never get to see the end result of their behind-the-scenes work, but this event offers a great opportunity for the whole team to share the joy.

- Pictures, pictures, and more pictures. This is a moment that you want people to remember for a long time to come. (And to post on their social pages!)

Group Discussion Questions

1. Why is having other people from the office participating in the Key Ceremony valuable for the homebuyer? Why is it valuable for the whole office?

2. How is communicating the Key Ceremony timing to other neighbors valuable to the new homeowner?

3. How can you make the Key Ceremony special for children or other members of the family?

Chapter Fifteen

Move-In Day

JANET HEADED TO KYLIE'S NEW HOME to help with the move-in. As she pulled up to Kylie's house, she noticed something unusual—a red carpet on the front porch that led through the front door and into the home. She was happy for Kylie, but her own personal disappointment only grew.

"Hi, there," said Kylie with a wave as she headed down the driveway. "Thanks for coming by. Oh my gosh, there is so much to do!"

"Happy to help. The red carpet is a nice touch."

"You missed the huge red bow on the front door," said Kylie. "It was so sweet!"

"I don't expect a red bow," replied Janet. "More likely a list of things still not completed tacked to the front door."

"Oh, come on, Janet. It'll be fine. I'm sure you'll be happy once you're moved in."

By noon the movers were placing furniture while Kylie and Janet began to unpack boxes in the kitchen. Janet noticed that one of the self-closing drawers was sticking.

"This drawer seems sticky to me," said Janet.

"Yeah, I noticed that," replied Kylie.

"Aren't you going to tell your superhuman construction team about that?"

"Well, the way the process works is that I note things that need to be looked at on a warranty form, and then I'll hand it in once I've completed the move-in. That way they can address everything at once."

"And you trust them to do that?" asked Janet.

"Certainly. They've pretty much followed through on all their promises to us."

The conversation was interrupted by Kylie's salesperson, entering the kitchen with a pizza in one hand and a bag of plates, napkins, and utensils in the other.

"Compliments of Matchless Homes, Kylie," said the salesperson with a smile. "We figured you had your hands full."

"You guys never cease to amaze me," said Kylie.

"Nor me," said a dejected Janet.

Homebuyer Insights

"We arrived at the home to see a beautiful basket on the kitchen counter full of essentials we might need on moving day. SO thoughtful…and it came in handy!"

Insights

Move-in day represents one of the most exciting—and simultaneously stressful—days in the entire process. It is a universal experience; the new homeowner has a thousand details to attend to.

Move-in day is a combination of joy and pain. No one likes to move—it's always stressful. But it is a lot more fun to unpack than to pack. The home builder's objective is to ensure that each homeowner's move-in experience is memorable, if not extraordinary!

This is an excellent occasion for "surprise and delight" moments. How can the team anticipate what the customer is going through, and how they can assist in making the move as painless as possible?

Move-in day surprise and delight opportunities don't have to be difficult. Little things make a huge impression. All you need to do is exceed your promises by a small amount to absolutely delight the buyer.

Homebuyer Insights

"Worst experience ever. I bought, sold, rented homes, and lived In military housing all over the world. This is by far the worst and dirtiest home we've ever moved into."

Setting Expectations

The first thing to remember is that every buyer expects the new home to be completely ready to move into. All the basics must work: water, HVAC, windows, doors, lights, plumbing. These "basics" are universally expected in a new home.

Of course, your customer satisfaction ratings will not be enhanced when these basic expectations are delivered.

Your reputation does not improve if the lock on the front door works as expected. No homeowner will run into the street and scream, "Thank you, (home builder name), MY TOILETS FLUSH PERFECTLY!"

However, you will pretty quickly hear about a non-functioning toilet. Non-functioning lights, water, or heat will always create dissatisfaction, and these issues are a death knell for homebuyer satisfaction ratings when they occur on or close to move-in day. The new homeowner's patience will certainly be tested when this happens…as will the thickness of your skin!

But nothing gets under the skin of a new homeowner more than finding something incomplete or inoperable without having been told about the problem in advance. Customers feel particularly angry when items identified as incomplete during the Orientation Tour are still in the same condition. Don't leave it to the customer to find the flaws. Total transparency is required in every phase, but particularly right before move-in: If you know that something is not complete or not in working order, prepare the homeowner *before* they show up for moving day.

Just prior to move-in day, homeowners should be reminded that although they will undoubtedly find a few things which either don't operate to their expectations, or were missed during the quality-control process, there is a clear and simple process for reporting such things. At the Orientation Tour and at the Key Ceremony, remind the homebuyer that these outstanding items will be resolved within 15 days, 30 days, 45 days, 60 days…the timing doesn't matter as long as you make a promise you know you will absolutely *beat*.

It bears repeating that customers do not offer rave reviews because promises are met, only when they are exceeded. Every customer care representative and every subcontractor who comes back out to the finished home must understand this and behave accordingly.

Homebuyer Insights

"Best part: The builder's amazingly kind people, including our great community friends and neighbors. When we pulled up to our home with our trailer, several neighbors walked from their homes to ours, to help move furniture and boxes into our home. Just amazing!"

Making the Move-In Extraordinary

Consider asking your Community Team a simple but powerful perspective. The question is this: What would impress *you* if you were the buyer?

Consider these ideas and best move-in day practices:

- Red carpet going up to the front entry

- A large red bow on the front door (no nails please!) with a sign or balloon that reads, *"Welcome to your new home!"*

- Get to the home early and leave a dozen freshly baked chocolate chip cookies. What a delicious aroma when the new homeowner opens the front door for the first time!

- Place a large basket of essentials on the kitchen counter: paper towels; toilet paper; sponges; bottled water; a touch-up paint brush; snacks; etc. Basically, the kinds of things you would want to have access to on moving day.

- Leave a list of local restaurants that can deliver today, with discount coupons the restaurant will be happy to provide to a potential new customer.

- Place a bottle of (screw-top) wine and clear plastic cups in an inexpensive cooler in the main bedroom, with a welcome note to the buyer from the salesperson.

- During move-in day, plan on unpromised visits from the salesperson, the superintendent, and the customer care representative. Each visitor can offer to carry a few boxes into the home.

- Task one of the visiting Community Team members with bringing over a large pizza just prior to lunch time.

- About two-thirds of your homeowners will have a pet. Bring over a new dog tag with the dog's name, the buyer's new address, and phone number.

- If it's raining or snowing, drop off plastic floor covering to protect the entryway floors. Leave a company branded umbrella (as a gift with a note from the customer service representative) next to the front door. Supply the customer with a few large but inexpensive towels and an extra roll of paper towels.

Home Builder How-To

On closing day we have their closing gift (cute doormat, stress relief candle, kitchen hand soap, hand towels, balloons, and cookies) in their home when they return from Title. We meet them at their new home with plenty of water for moving day and their keys to their new home!

Alisha Battle, New Home Advisor

Application

- Assign a team to brainstorm ideas for move-in day surprises. Make sure the ideas are cost-effective and easily repeatable. Roll out across all of your Community Teams and train accordingly.

- Consider ways to involve the neighbors. Encourage a healthy sense of community.

- If there's a problem that can be fixed easily, do it quickly. Taking care of the small things quickly shows the homeowner that you're attentive and efficient.

Eliant's research has shown that customers whose complaints were handled very quickly are more likely to provide higher ratings of their experience than customers who had no complaints at all!

Group Discussion Questions

1. How can you get neighborhood engagement on move-in day without invading privacy, being in the way, or otherwise being burdensome rather than helpful?

2. What are a few examples of the things that go awry on move-in day? What types of resources can you offer if something goes terribly wrong on move-in day?

3. Move-in day is a rite of passage for your Community Team too, not just the new homeowner. How do you make this a high-energy day filled with appreciation—and not just more work—for the organizational team too?

SECTION 4:

After
Move-In

Chapter Sixteen

Ongoing Customer Care

WHEN JANET ENTERED KYLIE'S HOUSE for a midday visit, she was not alone. Four different tradespeople were hard at work.

"What happened?" asked Janet to a relatively calm Kylie. "Who are all these people?"

"Well, we had a plumbing problem upstairs and water came leaking through the breakfast nook light fixture. We have a plumber working upstairs and two people repairing the paint and drywall where it leaked through. Then there's Kenneth, our customer care representative. He's coordinating the whole thing."

"When did this happen?" asked Janet.

"I was having breakfast and suddenly water started to drip onto my plate!"

"And you have this many people working on the issue already? That's impressive."

"Thank goodness for the emergency number," replied Kylie. "They were on it really quickly. Kenneth called it an 'all-hands-on-deck' moment. How are you and Matt getting along?"

"Not too bad," said Janet. "We still have a list of things that need to be completed and we have an ongoing problem with our backyard drainage. The way the grading was done leaves standing water against the foundation."

"Is it being addressed?" asked Kylie.

"Well, the builder swears they're 'working on it' but no one is communicating how long this is going to take, and I don't know if anyone has even been out to look at it yet. Matt's talking about bringing in an outside inspector. I just want it done."

"I get that," replied Kylie.

"And check this out. Our builder offered us $1,000 in cash if we refer someone to purchase at the community. Like I would sell out my friends for $1,000."

"We've already told several people about our builder," said Kylie. "Happy to do that. In fact, maybe you and Matt should sell your place and buy a home over here!"

"At this rate, anything's possible," replied Janet.

Homebuyer Insights

"This was an atrocious experience...the dishonesty and integrity of the company is disappointing, especially since I'm a licensed Realtor in the community that works with homebuilders daily."

Insights

What is the ultimate goal when it comes to providing outstanding customer care? What unites (or could unite) the entire team in a common mission—something tangible and measurable that would be a cause for celebration?

The big-picture goal for every employee in the organization should be to *earn referrals*. Referrals are the evidence of a strong team effort. A referral from a buyer should thus be celebrated as the significant achievement that it is. Referrals are the validation of a job well-performed!

The Recipe for Customer Care Success

To accomplish this objective, the team should maintain consistent focus on even the smallest elements of each customer's purchase and ownership experience. Very often, the smallest action—like leaving a 10-second voice mail message with a progress report—can make for significant owner appreciation.

Successful home builders look for small surprise and delight opportunities during this new phase of the customer's life. This could include fixing things that are clearly not covered by the warranty or embracing the opportunity several years after the move-in to repair an item which should have been done correctly during the construction phase. A number of Eliant's highest-ranked home builders formed customer care teams to quickly address out-of-warranty issues.

But it also means getting the fundamentals right. How a community team addresses customer issues is critical to overall satisfaction. Complaints and repair requests should not be viewed as troublesome events but as opportunities to exceed the homeowner's expectations.

According to joint research between Eliant and the USC Marshall School of Business, the three most important drivers of satisfaction when it comes to repairs are (in order):

1. Repairs completed right the first time

2. Service rep cleaned up after the repair

3. Speed of getting the issue fully resolved

If these factors are not already being measured, use this as your starting point.

Homebuyer Insights

"(Service tech) seems to genuinely care about our home and has the decency to come and see our issues in person. If something isn't covered, he communicates that in an honest but respectful manner."

Memorable Customer Care

The topic of ongoing customer care simply continues a theme that began prior to contract. The worst possible result is for a homeowner to believe that the builder stops caring once they've moved in. Communication and expectation-setting are just as important in the customer care phase as they were during the purchase experience. The phrase "under-promise and over-deliver" remains most appropriate for your Community Team mindset.

The Checklist for Memorable Customer Care:

1. Educate the Customer Early on How the Process Works

Prior to the move-in—and after providing the buyer with a *Personal Bio* of the customer care representative (see Chapter 5)—arrange for the homebuyer to meet the customer care representative face-to-face. Set the expectation that there will absolutely be occasions for contacting customer care, with questions or to correct something which may have been missed in the Orientation Tour or to repair something that went bad after the move-in.

Make sure the customer understands the specific process for communicating issues. For example:

"The customer care team looks forward to your call. You can call our customer care team or register your request at our on-line portal. If you leave a non-emergency message, someone will call you back within (24/48/72) hours."

As always, only promise a time you KNOW you can beat!

2. Quickly Confirm Receipt of the Repair Request

Homeowners are anxious to know that their issue will be resolved and that the home builder is aware of the problem. If it isn't possible to immediately return the customer's call, you must in some way let the homeowner know that the service request was received, and that someone will soon be in touch to answer questions or schedule an appointment. Use the customer's stated communication preference to decide if this confirmation should be communicated via text, email, or voice mail.

Remember the over-deliver rule. Call the home-owner within the promised time to arrange for the service appointment. If you promised a response within 24 hours, be sure to call back the same day or absolutely within 12 hours.

3. Schedule the Appointment as Early as Possible

As trivial as the homeowner's service issue may appear to you, the homeowner sees it as–serious enough to warrant a call to get it fixed. Keep in mind that the customer has to live with the issue every day until it's resolved. Whether it's a scratch in a cabi-net or an inoperable faucet, every time a customer looks at the problem it's another nagging reminder of incompletion.

One of the greatest improvements in a home builder's customer care process is to enable the cus-tomer to include a photo or video of the item along with their service request. These photos can then be forwarded to the customer care representative or trade partner. This eliminates confusion, possibly eliminates an initial "triage" visit, and gives the cus-tomer a greater sense of certainty that the problem is clearly understood.

Service request forms or portals should provide homeowners with an easy way to upload a photo(s).

4. Schedule a Triage Visit (when necessary)

Lacking photos or sufficient details about the problem, many builders send their customer care representative to the home to triage or assess the issue and determine next steps. This clearly adds another visit to the home, which can be viewed by homeowners as bothersome. The trade-off, however, is that the trade's service technician will be better prepared to complete the repair in one visit.

5. Provide an Appointment Time Window

Many homeowners must use workplace vacation time to be at home for the service visit. And they may have arranged to pick up their kids before or after your promised appointment time. Showing up at the promised time is certainly important to the homeowner's schedule and will yield satisfaction, but this timely arrival will not *delight* your customer.

On the other hand, a late arrival, particularly if arrival status is not properly communicated, can be devastating to the homeowner's impression of your reliability and your commitment to customers.

Follow these steps to ensure a positive service appointment:

- The appointment time window is typically two hours in length, a timespan most customers find reasonable.

- Ideally, customers should receive an "Appointment Confirmation" email or text 24 hours in advance of the appointment. *(If your dentist can do this, why can't you?)*

- Require your technician or trade representative to call or text the homeowner 30 to 60 minutes prior to arrival.

- If the technician or trade rep expects to be delayed past the promised window, the homeowner should be called at least two hours in advance to communicate this probable delay.

6. Make a Good Impression at Arrival

Homeowners "size up" your customer care representative or trade technicians within 10 to 15 seconds! Here are a few simple steps for creating a positive first impression of the rep's sincere interest in caring for the customer's home:

- Never park in the driveway. That is the homeowner's private space and must be protected from oil leaking from your service vehicle.

- Always put on clean booties at the front door (even if your shoes are clean).

- Carry a small blanket to protect the floor or other surfaces (even if you have no intention of using it).

- Carry a hand vac (even if you have no intention of using it).

- Carry small towels to clean up after the repair.

- Wear a name tag with a logo (with first name in large letters).

- SMILE as you introduce yourself to the homeowner.

- Use a breath mint prior to approaching the home.

- NEVER smoke within one hour of a service visit.

7. Communicate the Resolution or Next Steps

Show the customer what was done to resolve the issue. Take before and after photos of the repair for record-keeping and dispute resolution.

If for some reason the repair cannot be completed, share a clear course of action for your customer, explaining what will happen next, and providing a timeline for completion. And SMILE while doing so!

Homebuyer Insights

"Annoyed by tradespeople showing up on the wrong day!"

Dealing with the Inevitable Problems

Things are going to go wrong, sometimes very wrong. Disputes will arise. Homeowners will be victims of their own expectations. We're dealing with peoples' homes; we can often expect an emotional response. Too many builder representatives fail to understand the emotional toll that problems can take on homeowners. Empathy is a must in these situations.

In face-to-face or telephone discussions with a complaining or angry homeowner, here is the **"5-Step Dispute Resolution Procedure"** recommended by psychologists:

1. Use Active Listening techniques as the customer is complaining (head nods, eye contact, hmm, mm-hmm, *"I understand"*)

2. Restate what you heard (so the customer recognizes that you clearly understand the issue)

3. Empathize (*"This must be difficult on your family…"*)

4. Apologize

5. State intended action plan to resolve this issue

Once the homebuyer becomes a homeowner, customer care immediately becomes the primary driver of customer satisfaction and future sales from customer referrals. If the purchase experience covers the first 8½ innings of the ball game, customer care is the bottom of the ninth. All the credits you've earned until that point can be lost with a single poor servicing of the customer's needs after move-in.

It's also true that incredible customer service can reclaim some of the customer's loyalty when the purchase experience was not all that positive. However, a negative customer service experience is more powerful, more impactful on homeowner satisfaction than a positive experience. In other words, you have more to lose than to gain.

There is much at stake, but there's also a magnificent consequence of a job well done: a possible sale from a homeowner's referral and a subsequent team celebration!

Home Builder How-To

If a customer is only hearing from you when there's bad news, how is that going to make them feel when they see your name pop up on their phone or when an email chimes through? The last thing you want is for someone to associate your business with a negative feeling.

Kaylie Austin, Division Sales Manager

Application

- Set sales-from-referrals targets and track them.

- Consider compensation adjustments for Community Team members based on customers' scores on the

"Willingness to Recommend My Builder" question
on your customer experience questionnaires.

• Write your warranty and correction procedures *from
the customer's point of view*. Always be asking how the
home builder's "policy" affects the customer's overall
experience.

• Make the parameters clear when it comes to what
will and will not be done to satisfy a customer's issue
or concern.

• Go through the checklist above and make sure every
team member and trade partner understands the specific steps of a memorable customer care experience.

Group Discussion Questions

1. Anything that happens after the actual close and
   move-in day might seem anti-climactic for your
   Community Team. How do you keep energy and
   responsiveness high?

2. How well is your team prepared for an "all-hands-on-
   deck" moment? Can they and will they drop everything to be on-site as needed for an emergency?

3. What are the best ways to ensure that the homebuyer
   always has the customer care contact information at
   their fingertips?

Chapter Seventeen

Preparing for the Customer Evaluation Process

KYLIE COULDN'T HELP BUT NOTICE the home builder survey form on Janet's kitchen table. She knew that the experience that Janet and Matt had was not good, so she approached the conversation cautiously.

"Have you filled it out yet?" she asked.

Janet was snarky in her reply. "Well, they certainly gave me the specific instructions on how to do that—just give them all 10s. Like *that* would ever happen."

"Wait, they asked for perfect scores? I mean, they had to know you had a less-than-perfect experience."

"Oh, it's worse than that," replied Janet. "The superintendent told us that he gets a bonus with better results, so if we give him good scores, he'll do some extra stuff for us."

"Does that mean that if you give him low scores, he'll ignore you?" asked Kylie.

"Well, he's certainly well-practiced in ignoring, so I suppose that wouldn't surprise me. Have you filled yours out?"

"We were happy to do so," replied Kylie. "Our salesperson just asked us to be honest about the experience. They use the information to get better."

Janet sighed. "Honestly, I don't think anyone really cares about our opinion on the process. So I'm going to ignore the survey, write a letter to the company owner, and then just tell everyone I know not to buy from this builder."

"Ouch," said Kylie.

"Yeah, ouch. You just described our entire experience in a single word."

Homebuyer Insights

"I have been surprisingly happy with the customer service. With so many homes going up I thought how will they have time to take care of things I need, but customer service has met all my expectations and more."

Insights

Let's restate a premise that was offered in the prologue of this book. The best home builders are not looking for great scores; they're looking to provide great experiences that *earn* great scores.

The survey itself is a truth-telling mechanism. If administered correctly, it provides an accurate depiction of the customer's journey and a road map for how to improve. Attempting to manipulate a customer into giving a high score defeats the very purpose of the survey in the first place.

A New Description

With that in mind, let's change the paradigm with this suggestion: Eliminate the word "survey" from your organizational vocabulary and replace it with "evaluation."

Think about the objective here. We're asking the customer to evaluate the purchase and ownership journey from his or her unique perspective. A survey speaks more to preferences; an evaluation speaks more to experiences.

This is perhaps a minor distinction, but Eliant's research confirms that homeowners are more likely to respond to our invitation to participate if we ask them to *evaluate* their experience and provide their suggestions for improvement instead of being asked to "fill out a survey."

Homebuyer Insights

"Customer service is non-responsive to my emails and phone calls."

Motivation for the Evaluation

Many home builders beg and plead with a homeowner to participate in completing a survey. Instead, we would do better by asking why a homeowner would want to take part in this process in the first place. Homebuyers and homeowners are more likely to complete and return their evaluations under the following circumstances:

1. They are either VERY satisfied or VERY dissatisfied with their experience. Response rates increase when buyers come closer to either end of the satisfaction spectrum.

2. They feel obligated due to the relationship(s) they formed with at least one of the team members.

3. They're eager to share specific comments and suggestions about their experience.

4. They view this evaluation process as part of their overall experience with your company. This is a belief that the builder must foster and stimulate by telling each buyer—at contract—that there is a "partnership" between the home builder and homebuyer, and that part of the homebuyer's obligation to the builder is to provide his or her opinion of the experience.

Home Builder How-To

The time to prepare for the survey is before the purchase. The survey score will be great if you care more about the customer journey than you do about the survey. Even with a perfect score, a negative comment feels like a failure. We evaluate every score and every comment, look at our systems, and see how we can change our systems to prevent problems in the future.

John Upchurch, Vice President of Sales and Marketing

Driving Higher Response Rates

Eliant has identified a series of specific behaviors that equate to higher response rates on evaluations. Use this as a checklist for your own efforts.

- Start with the basics. Ensure that team members focus on delivering and improving the key "Referral Driver Behaviors" in their department. Successful builders provide continual training for improving each representative's performance on these Referral Driver Behaviors. And OH…delighted customers are more likely to complete their evaluation!

- Remind buyers that the management team reviews every evaluation and uses this information to constantly improve their processes in every phase of the experience.

- Create and consistently maintain performance-based bonus plans to a large degree based on performance on these Referral Drivers and the Willingness to Refer score.

- Create and maintain team member recognition programs for those with the highest evaluation results.

- Train each of the team members to introduce the customer evaluation process in the same way, using the same language and consistent terminology.

- Create a "customer-focused culture" in which each team member is excited to receive customer feedback. The team should look at negative evaluations as a gift, an opportunity to learn how to improve.

- Talk about customers' comments or evaluation ratings in every meeting. Team members will become interested in the ratings and comments when their leaders show active interest.

- Share copies of the survey questions with each manager and team member so they understand the behaviors they're expected to demonstrate. (*"These are the criteria on which you will be evaluated."*)

- Set clear rules for how team members should introduce the customer evaluation process: no gaming the system; we need honest and unskewed ratings and comments. Honest comments and suggestions allow us to use this information to improve.

- Field representatives must never challenge a customer who gave less than desired ratings. Buyers do not want to be confronted about their ratings and will never again complete your future evaluations if they're challenged for describing their perception. Only managers should be contacting low-scoring customers to learn more about the reasons for the customers' dissatisfaction.

Home Builder How-To

We do touchpoint surveys throughout the buyer's journey. We're attempting to provide real-time metrics to the sentiment of our buyer at each segment of the process to determine subtle dissatisfaction in the moment. This will allow us to provide corrective measures proactively versus through the 60-day or 180-day post-settlement surveys which are true lagging indicators, leaving us very little we can do to turn that customer around at that point.

We're using smiley face surveys that are one-click responses with the ability for the lead and eventual buyer to provide a green, yellow, or red marker. They can also provide a written explanation.

Brooks Sears, Director of Sales

The Big Six Referral Drivers

Each year, Eliant conducts over 200,000 evaluations of home-buyer and homeowner perceptions of their new home purchase and ownership experience. Average response rates on these different types of evaluations range from 70% immediately after the move-in (with many builders reaching over 80%) to 46% after one year in the home. With such a high customer response rate, Eliant is able to achieve unusually strong levels of statistical validity in testing the causal relationship between each question on the customer evaluations and the primary question asked of every customer: *"How willing are you to recommend your builder to a friend or family member?"*

Eliant provides the data from its homeowner evaluations to the University of Southern California (USC) Marshall School of Business. Graduate student classes then
conduct a large number of statistical analyses, including
regression analysis. Based on these analyses, here are the
six builder-staff behaviors that have the strongest impact
on consumers' willingness to recommend their builder to
a friend or family member. There's at least one behavior
from each of the builder's departments:

1. **Salespeople**: The frequency with which the salesperson keeps the buyer informed of construction
   progress *before the buyer has to ask*. (During the
   contract-to-close period, this is the #1 driver of willingness to recommend the builder!)

2. **Design Selection Advisors:** The ability of the
   designer to *sell the value* of the design selection experience, even though prices are often higher than can
   be found in local retail stores or on-line. (e.g. additional warranty; counseling or advice on products,
   model differentiation, colors, etc.)

3. **Loan Officers:** The frequency with which the loan
   officer or processor keeps the buyer informed of loan
   and documentation status *before the buyer has to ask*.

4. **Construction Superintendent:** Job site cleanli-
   ness. (i.e. buyers who cannot view the home's interior

assume the home is being constructed with quality if the job site is clean and orderly.)

5. Home Delivery: The delivery of the home on the promised date, complete and clean.

6. Warranty Service and Customer Care: Repairs completed right-the-first-time. And repair site is left clean.

The fastest way to create improved levels of customer delight and referral likelihood is to include the appropriate Referral Driver(s) in each department's "Performance-Bonus" plan.

Application

- Leaders must create a culture where every evaluation is appreciated and respected as a way to both commend superior performance or find ways to improve. There should be nothing punitive in our response to poor evaluations. These are learning opportunities.

- Eliminate any negative or undesired practices from your current operation. Examples: Failing to prepare the homeowner for the evaluation. Begging for good scores. Ignoring the lessons.

- Use the response rate checklist (above) as a guide for internal training.

Group Discussion Questions

1. How do you thank homebuyers for providing timely and thoughtful customer evaluation responses?

2. How can you use customer evaluation responses to find and address areas of opportunity for improvement? What systems are in place to ensure that process improvement is the result of a survey response?

3. What would you do if one of your departments disagreed with the data coming from customer evaluations?

4. If you constantly receive very high satisfaction in one or more functional areas, how do you keep motivation high?

Chapter Eighteen

Earning Referrals

JANET LOOKED ACROSS THE TABLE and made a stark observation to Kylie.

"Here's the difference between you and me. We're both talking about the experience we had with our home builders, and we're both doing it with the same level of passion. But the nature of the experience makes for two very different stories."

Kylie replied, "Completely agree. Frankly, I want people to experience what Craig and I went through. That's how pleased we are."

"And I want people to avoid our home builder at all costs; that's how unhappy we are," said Janet.

"But I thought you loved your home, Janet."

"We do. We love the floor plan and the livability. But the experience just wasn't worth it. We feel something of a duty to warn other people."

"Fair enough," replied Kylie. "Sorry you had to go through all that. But let's move on. I have some ideas about the nursery and I'd love to get your opinion."

"I'd love to, Kylie. This is what it's all about. Let's do it right!"

Homebuyer Insights

"We submitted four pages in response to your first survey and no one ever contacted us to discuss it so I have to assume you really aren't interested in our thoughts on the experience."

Insights

There are two objectives here, one simple and one complex. The simple task is to ask for a referral; the complex task is to earn it in the first place.

Let's be clear on one thing. A lousy experience makes the referral request needless. In fact, requesting a referral from an angry buyer will likely blow up in your face.

That said, there's always an opportunity to redeem the situation, to get back into the owner's good graces, and *then* to ask for the referral. An extraordinary, over-the-top customer service experience can potentially salvage a horrible purchase experience.

The Ask

The referral request, while simple, must be well-crafted and well-rehearsed. There's an art to asking for a referral so that it comes across as conversational. There should be no sense of obligation on your customer's part, but rather an acknowledgment that the service provided was worth celebrating.

A poorly constructed referral request might sound some-thing like this:

> *"We sure appreciate referrals. Is there someone you know who's looking to purchase?"*

That approach is blunt, cold, and self-serving. Think about asking in a way that's far more cooperative and conversational.

> *"It's been our pleasure to be on this journey with you. One of the great things about buy-ing a brand-new home is that you can literally choose your own neighbors. Is there someone who comes to mind who might be interested in living in this community?"*

As we've been saying throughout, practice, practice, practice! You want the referral request to be easy and fluid.

Homebuyer Insights

"OMG! I can't say enough about our agent. I would say he's the main reason we purchased a lot and home here. He stuck with us through every step to insure we got what we wanted...always smiling. Always happy. Can't wait to have him over for dinner."

The Timing

The request for a referral should not be a one-and-done occurrence. Customers need to be reminded from time to time. Before we get to the specific timing of the referral request, there's an overriding rule of thumb to consider: Feel free to ask for a referral whenever the customer is clearly happy with your performance. Strike while the emotional iron is hot. That's when the customer will be most likely to give the question some serious consideration.

Beyond that, referral requests should be milestone driven, specifically when considering the moments of high Emotional Altitude. You don't have to ask at each of the points listed below, but each of these milestone moments represent times of high Emotional Altitude:

- Pre-Contract. Yes, *before* the contract is signed. As soon as the salesperson feels confident the prospect is seriously considering a purchase, they can ask for the referral by using the format above. Extra benefit: The request may even give the prospect an additional rationale to finalize the purchase decision. ("I can get my two friends to live here as well, WOW!")

- Point of Contract. Definitely a time when customers are in tune to their future, and the relationship with the home builder is solid.

- Design Selection. This is the fun part. Strike while the emotional iron is the hottest.

- Frame Walk or Orientation Tour. Assuming the process has been enjoyable, this is the payoff.

- Closing Appointment. Customers are excited about their new home and thinking already about their new life. Give them the opportunity to make the neighborhood better by having friends and family move in.

- 30 Days After Move-In. Now that they love their home and the boxes are unpacked, why not get them thinking about who else might be interested?

- 90-Day Intervals Thereafter. Think about how your CRM system can remind you to ask for referrals.

Homebuyer Insights

"I am living in paradise!! Best decision my wife and I ever made."

Whom To Ask

There are buyers for whom the referral request should be avoided, and then there are easily identifiable buyers who can be targeted to ask for their referral(s). In addition to the salesperson's judgment, you can use customers' evaluation scores to determine who should be high on the list of targeted customers from which referrals are most likely.

Who makes the call? The team member who's closest to the customer, typically the salesperson:

> *"Hi, Jenny, this is Marsha Johnson. How are you? I'm calling because I just read the evaluation you submitted on Monday. It sounds like you were quite pleased with your purchase experience, and I wanted to thank you for your kind words. It made me very happy to read that!*
>
> *"It's been our pleasure to be on this journey with you. Thank you for trusting us to build your home and take care of you along the way. One of the great things about buying a brand-new home is that you can literally choose your own neighbors. Is there someone who comes to mind who might be interested in living in this community? We would love to reach out to him or her."*

Homebuyer Insights

"I have a suggestion. Fix my house first. THEN you can proceed to beg for me to tell others how "great" you are."

Referral Incentives

Our clients have had great success with offering "Referral Incentives" to those homebuyers and homeowners who referred a friend, but only if the customer's buying experience was positive. Both the current customer and the referred buyer should earn some type of incentive. This can be an Amazon gift certificate, a gift certificate to a local store or restaurant chain (www.giftcertificates.com), or a credit at the home builder's design studio.

The real beauty of the referral-incentive program is that it gives the salesperson an excuse to call current customers to (1) inform them of the new incentive program or changes to the current program, and (2) ask for the referral.

Home Builder How-To

"I tease my homeowners if they haven't sent a referral my way. I believe I've earned the right to ask and to ask consistently."

Laura Oakley, Sales Representative

Action Items

- Script out your referral requests and come up with several different versions.

- Brainstorm some clever collateral pieces that would add value to the customer while making it clear that referrals are appreciated.

- Consider a small gift for each referral received, whether that referred person buys or not. This is a great way to encourage still more referrals.

Group Discussion Questions

1. What could happen if you ask for a referral from a customer who is not on the satisfied end of the spectrum?

2. How do you or can you celebrate with your Community Team when referrals are received?

3. At what point in a customer's home buying journey do you get the most referrals? (If you don't have this data, what can you do to ensure you'll get it in the future?)

Epilogue

THE STORY OF KYLIE AND JANET is, of course, a fable. But we suspect that it didn't take much imagination for industry veterans to see a whole lot of real life in the tale.

We love and celebrate the stories of Kylie and Craig. We also cringe and find ourselves embarrassed about the stories of Janet and Matt (even if most of us are guilty of similar experiences we offered at some point in our careers!)

But perhaps we have the wrong perspective on these takeaways. What if we were to lean into and celebrate the tough ones? What if we changed our very paradigm about complaints and customer challenges?

Great customer experience organizations know something that other companies don't. Every customer journey that goes sour is an opportunity to get better.

The irony of our fable is that we don't have a lot to learn from Kylie and Craig's incredible experience. The lessons come from the difficulties encountered by Janet and Matt—if we're willing to listen and learn. There are lessons to be learned in the face of adversity that you cannot learn in the comfort of victory.

To that end, we challenge you to lean into the mistakes and failed expectations and listen attentively to the customers who complain…or simply describe their misadventures.

Gather your team every month and read all your customers' survey comments aloud. Trust that every complaint is that customer's wish that your team will improve the experience delivered to future customers.

Our goal is not that you would simply feel enlightened having read this book, but rather that you feel *activated*. Take it upon yourself—regardless of your role in the organization—to own the care of your customers. Be a ringleader. Be an advocate.

As Gandhi suggested, "Be the change you wish to see in the world." (OK, OK…we know that Gandhi didn't *really* say exactly that. But let's pretend that he did and live by it anyway!)

Now go out there and change someone's world!